FUCKERY

THE LIFE AND TIMES
OF A LEGEND
(IN HER OWN MIND)

JUDI HARRINGTON

Fuckery / Judi Harrington—1st ed.

Paperback ISBN 978-1-956989-04-5
Hardcover ISBN978-1-956989-05-2

Contents

A Word from the Author

On the day I was born, five planets were in retrograde. My astrology friends tell me this planetary phenomenon explains everything about who I am.

Perhaps the following stories will reveal that answer for you, dear reader, because it remains a mystery to me.

You've probably seen women who move through the world in a state of perpetual ease and grace. Their hair is smooth yet bouncy. An ideal parking spot always opens up, just in time for their arrival. Their children speak fluent French and conversational Japanese and enjoy folding laundry. For these people, the stars align in harmonious precision.

I am not one of these people. For me, life is an embodiment not of the stars' alignment but rather fuckery.

Fuckery (Fuh–Ker–Ree)
noun
1. Pertains to a person, situation (or place) that
   is considered ridiculous or nonsensical
2. An alternative to the word "bullshit"
3. Judi Harrington's favorite curse word

Origin:
Jamaican slang word

This Jamaican Patois term was first introduced to American mainstream/pop culture in a scene from the movie "(top) Shottas," which can be heard during the deportation interrogation scene.

"You're one of them from foreign, who commit all of the crimes. Then you come back here to mash up the island with your foreign style car jacking extortion, all types of fuckery!"

- Jamaican officer to protagonist Biggs in 'Shottas'
Source: The Urban Dictionary

While I must admit I've never been involved in a carjacking (of course, the day is young!), I know that fuckery comes in many forms, as evidenced by my entire life.

A Statement on Accuracy

Everything in this book is true or, at least, mostly true as far as my middle-aged, menopausal mind can remember.

Or, as the author Michael Chabon writes in his novel, *Mysteries of Pittsburgh*:

"No doubt all of this is not true remembrance but the ruinous work of nostalgia, which obliterates the past, and no doubt, as usual, I have exaggerated everything."

You decide, dear reader. You decide.

Finally, all the names of people mentioned in these stories are, in fact, their real names. So if you are reading along and see your name, yes, it's you. You might be a main character, you might make a cameo appearance, but I assure you, it's you.

No Sickness, Only Health

Moms can never get sick. NEVER. And the minute they do, all family operations come to a screeching halt because, suddenly, no one knows how to do anything without Mom. You could have a house full of MENSA members, but if Mom gets sick, no one can add 1+1, and everyone is a self-proclaimed illiterate. No child prodigy ever cracked a code when Mom was sick.

Such was my predicament today, or rather, the night before, when my husband declared that he had planned a very special and romantic date night for us. Or, more accurately, he told his friend, Aidan, "Let's go out for beers. Maybe bring the wives." From my husband's lips, this statement was equivalent to roses, champagne, and a bathtub filled with honeyed milk! Swoon!

In a state of erotic rapture, I booked a sitter. But all plans got kicked to the curb when suddenly, I had a scratchy throat. Thinking I was just thirsty, I made some herbal tea. Then the coughing started. And it wouldn't stop.

Mick came out from his shower, dressed for a "night out," which, for an Irishman, means, "I am wearing jeans I did not go to work in and a shirt that I bought sometime in the past decade."

"Wow, you have a cough," he noted as I hacked gobs of phlegm and gurgled in agony.

As much as I wanted to scream, "NO KIDDING!!" I refrained. Mick is understated by nature, and there was a tinge of sympathy in his voice. Or was it a shock to him that I wasn't well since I rarely get sick? Who knows? As the resident International Man of Mystery, speculating on his true meaning and intention could be an all-day event.

Choosing to view his statement as an act of sympathy, I reciprocated with kindness. After all, he did initiate our plans.

"Yes, I do. I'm hoping I can rally through dinner because I really want to go out."

"What's for dinner?"

"The kids can have pasta. They can even make it, or the babysitter can."

Yes, my kids cook. My style of mothering involves teaching life skills, and cooking is top of the list. I'm not cultivating the next Alice Waters or even the next Rachel Ray, but I do know that our children can make grilled cheese or pasta.

Fast forward 30 minutes: The cough is no better. I am slowly moving through the stages of grief. I am the kind of person who will go out to attend the opening of an envelope, so for me to cancel plans, you know I cannot be well.

After languishing in the Land of Denial and touching upon the Berth of Bargaining, I fast-forwarded to Acceptance and canceled our plans. Of course, this prompted Mick to ask, "What's for dinner now that we aren't going out?"

"Eat pasta. Make a sandwich. I can't think about food right now."

I went to bed, where I spent the rest of the evening reading and trying various "polite elixirs" that meant to show us that Big Pharma is totally unnecessary but really are designed for moms who know that the minute they get sick is the minute that every OTC medication in their house is expired. Such was the case in my house, and by now, my family was glued to the television watching the Pats. This left me to try quelling my cough with the following, in no particular order:

- Vicks Vaporub on my feet, with fuzzy socks on over them.
- Honey, ginger, lemon, and hot water.
- Honey, ginger, lemon, garlic, and hot water.
- Garlic, lemon, and hot water.
- Cinnamon and honey in hot water.

Just. Make. The. Damn. Eggs."

Everyone stopped in their tracks, for we had entered into our very own valley of the shadow of death, complete with the vintage McLaughlin sign that the end of times is near.

I burst into tears.

The only thing worse than when Mom is sick is when Mom demonstrates human emotion.

Especially if that mom is me.

I retreated back to the couch. Mick supervised as the girls made eggs but not without collateral damage: a broken salsa jar. Of course, I could have lived the rest of my life not knowing about that incident, but Ruth ratted out her father.

I don't believe in favorite children, but believe me: If I did, she would win that title today.

The suffering continued when I reminded the family that we were scheduled to go to "Family Faith Formation" at church. Think Sunday School with the whole family. I have already announced I am not going.

Mick says, "Oh, that's today?"

I pause, take a deep breath, and say, "Yes, it is today. That was why I said last night, 'Can't stay out too late because we have Generations of Faith tomorrow.' That's also why I have it posted on the fridge. That's also why I said, 'Wow, this weekend is booked with all sorts of stuff, including GOF on Sunday!'"

"What is Ruth going to eat at Generations of Faith?"

Aside from the fact that Ruth just made eggs and probably wasn't hungry, GOF starts with a meal. Ruth has celiac. She has had it since 2008. This means that she has to bring her own meal since she is more than likely allergic to the one that is being served.

This also means that Ruth's celiac is not news to Mick.

To boot, Mick has already been to the grocery store and purchased enough gluten-free food to feed a small nation. Hence, in theory, he would know what to give her.

But not if Judi is sick.

"She can have chicken fingers."

"She had some last night."

"She can have them again today."

While Mick was making chicken fingers (again!), I called My Sapphic Spouse, Amy-Jayne. She would know how to help me. First, she listened to my tales of woe, then she brought me REAL MEDICATION!!! And she was smart enough to bring them when my family had left so we could talk about them undisturbed.

Today's added bonus? She told me, "Wow! You look like shit!"

Amy-Jayne parted, and I proceeded to slip into a medicated sleep until my family decided to come home and ruin my life again some more. Bless them; they are consistent.

"What are we going to have for dinner?"

"Pretend I'm dead. You'll figure something out. You know what? Go to the 5 p.m. Mass; they have bread there."

"Ru can't have that bread."

"Ru hasn't asked at all today what she is going to eat. That's because she probably figured it out!"

"No, she asked me to ask you."

"Please, for the love of all that is holy and unholy, in the name of Jesus and Mary and all the angels and saints, leave me alone. Go forth and figure shit out."

Mick and Ru leave for Mass. Zoe managed to stay behind and make popcorn for herself. Not because she is self-sufficient, but because she knows this is probably the only time I will let her just eat whatever she can get into the microwave and I won't care.

But of course, she has to come up and "check on me."

"How are you feeling, Mama?"

"Like poop, Zo."

"Can I have your blanket?"

"No, Zo."

"Aw."

"Please, go watch TV, Zo."

Mick and Ru return from Mass with takeout. Vietnamese chicken pho for me, and whatever-the-hell-they-wanted for them.

Ru joins me on the couch for dinner and proceeds to tell me that Dada said something "nice" about me. When she said "nice," she invoked the air quotes we've all become accustomed to in our generation.

"He said he hopes you get better. He also said he hopes you don't give it to us."

"Don't worry, honey. I won't be giving anything to your father for a LONG TIME."

And that, dear friends, is how I came to appreciate that adage, "Every wife needs a wife," which I have expanded to include, "And every sick wife definitely needs a healthy wife."

Let us pray that there is NEVER a virus that specifically targets moms because then the entire planet is fucked.

The World's Most Approachable Woman

For a pair of Depression-era babies, Billy and Mary Harrington were ahead of their time in that they were "burn your television" people long before it became trendy. As my brother wrote in the dedication of his first book:

"...[T]o my mother, Mary Harrington, who thought a library card was a better entertainment system than a video game console."

Reading was the preferred pastime of the Harrington Family, with the local library holding as much esteem as the Catholic Church. Whereas our mother ensured our weekly attendance at Mass, our father ensured we made a weekly pilgrimage to the hallowed halls of the Fall River Public Library.

Daddy was a celebrity at the library, not only for his flirtatious manner with the staff but in that he was the most voracious reader they'd ever met. No matter the topic—mysteries, true crime, history, religion, politics—our father was known by one and all for his ability to rip through two or three 500-page books a week.

We were expected to follow suit.

"You can take out as many books as you can carry home, no matter what topic. But you damn well better read them" was Daddy's signature send-off before he turned to the stacks in search of his own literary escape.

And so we did.

Charlie was obsessed with dinosaurs, so he grabbed as many of those books as he could. I read through all of the Encyclopedia Brown series and then took on Nancy Drew and The Hardy Boys.

I loved the nuggets of knowledge I picked up as the characters solved mysteries.

Then came *The Guinness Book of World Records*, which introduced me to the concept that "firsts" and superlatives applied to people. The man with the longest fingernails. The tallest woman. The first man to travel at G-force speed. I was enraptured and remember scoring my very own copy somewhere, somehow, and reading it from cover to cover, over and over again. It sat on my nightstand and served as my bedtime lullaby.

Little did I know that someday I would earn the nickname of The World's Most Approachable Woman.

Perhaps it's an outward manifestation of all the quirky knowledge I absorbed as a child. Still, there is a phenomenon with me whereby I am forever the person strangers choose to ask for directions, take a picture, or, if I'm incredibly fortunate, tell me their life story.

In short, I could be standing in Times Square on New Year's Eve, and someone will choose me from the cast of thousands and ask for directions to Central Park.

Or what time it is.

Or if I know who will be performing next.

The phenomenon was first dubbed Nurse's Face by my friend Lucia, who observed that no matter where we were, people picked me out of a crowd to ask for help in some way, shape, or form. She said it was because I have a kind face, the kind that a nurse would have.

"Nurse Ratched?"

"No, silly, a nice nurse!"

No matter how I try to disguise myself, Jackie O sunglasses, hats, hoodies—believe me, I've tried!—I am approached by strangers far and wide for assistance.

I could have earphones on, face buried in *The Anarchist Cookbook*, and still, I get asked things like, "Do you know how to get to the airport from here?" or "Do you know where the Baptist church is?"

And here's the kicker: I almost always know the answer and end up providing it because I don't like to be rude.

Well, and these people won't leave me alone even if I was.

I am also often mistaken for the person in charge no matter where I go. I worked as a paralegal for many years, and more often than not, I was mistaken for the attorney when clients came in for appointments. Some friends have insisted I am an attorney. I have also been mistaken for a doctor while at the hospital (visiting), an engineer while at city hall (getting a parking pass), and a professor (when I was a graduate student).

I was traveling on a flight recently, and as I was storing my bag in the overhead bin, someone asked me, "Is this flight full?"

"I am not with the crew."

"Are you sure?"

See? People really want to believe I am in charge.

Last summer, I was on the MBTA Blue Line, and as the door opened, I heard someone ask, "Does this train go to the airport?"

The person asking was looking directly at me. I was not the sole occupant of the train car. There were about 30 people there, including my own family and friends, but no, she chose me.

"Sure does! All aboard!" I replied, resigned to my role as Our Lady of Perpetual Beacon of Knowledge.

Or, as my friend, Dan, dubbed me a few years ago, "Judi 411."

Now for you young folk, the "411" reference may be dated, so allow me a brief sidebar to explain: Many moons ago, before we were all tethered to technology, if you wanted someone's phone number, you often called "Information" by dialing "411."

As a walking information booth, Dan felt 411 was an apt term. And lo and behold, it stuck.

While my friends and family find the 411 phenomenon amusing, I myself am baffled. What most people don't know is that my dream in life is to live hiding in plain sight, the way the infamous criminal Whitey Bulger did for years before his capture.

Alas, I will not enjoy anonymity in this lifetime.

A few weeks ago, I was walking to the train in Davis Square in Somerville during rush hour, and a woman approached me to ask how to get to Tufts University.

"I will tell you if you answer me one question."

"Sure."

Dramatically sweeping my arm to show her the vast number of humans amongst us, I asked, "Why, out of all these people on the street, did you approach me?"

"You look like you know what's going on. You look knowledgeable."

"But I have these big glasses on; how can you see my face?"

"It's how you carry yourself. You are confident."

"Two blocks up the street on the left is the beginning of campus. Have a nice day."

My enlightened persona evidently knows no bounds because it seems I also look knowledgeable when I am breastfeeding an infant in Faneuil Hall.

Yes, dear reader, the most outrageous example of The Judi 411 Phenomenon revolves around me in precisely that position.

I was en route to a dentist appointment in downtown Boston, my infant daughter, Zoe, tucked in a stroller. Prior to her debut as the poster child for Extreme Separation Anxiety (a tale I will save for another day), I was able to bring Zoe along to dental cleanings thanks to the office manager, Lisa, who would watch her for me. With about 20 minutes to spare, Zoe had begun to fuss, so I parked my rear on a bench outside Faneuil Hall and began my ninja moves as a discreet breastfeeder.

And before anyone starts with "you should have no shame in breastfeeding a baby in public!"—I know. Again, I don't want attention from strangers. Re-read the above if you are unclear on this point.

Anyway…

About five minutes into feeding, a gentleman approached and started to get into my personal space. He was holding a phone to his ear, and just as we were about to butt foreheads, I said, "Can I help you?" in my most irritated voice.

He stepped back, extended his arm with the phone in it, which we all know as the universal signal for "Please talk to them."

The signature element of Judi 411 is that I am completely unfazed by weirdness. I took the phone.

"Um, hello?"

"Hi, yes, the man who gave you the phone found it. It's mine. He doesn't speak any English, and I need to get my phone."

Of course, you do.

"Okay, well, he's outside Faneuil Hall. He's a black male about five foot nine, wearing a blue shirt and jeans."

"Where's Faneuil Hall?"

Of course, you are a tourist. Of course.

"Near the Government Center T stop."

"We are at Ashmont, and we don't know the city."

Of course, I have to give you directions.

"Okay, you'll need to ask one of the MBTA attendants how to get to Government Center, but once you arrive, go upstairs, and he will be standing there with your phone."

"How do you know?"

"Because I will tell him."

"But he only speaks French."

"Today is your lucky day. So do I."

So yes, I gave the man directions in French to go to Government Center and stood there with the phone over his head.

I don't mind helping the lost, the confused, the hapless. Really. I don't. In fact, it often feels good to provide directions or translation services. However, for just one blessed day of my life, I would love to spend 24 hours without having someone tug at my sleeves to say, "Can you help?" or "Do you work here?"

I have a plan. I'll stay home. Curtains drawn. Lights off. Perhaps a ferocious guard dog to ward off intruders. But even as I map it out, I know my plan will fail.

Just as I'm tucking myself deep beneath a mountain of pillows for a luxurious Netflix binge, the doorbell rings. A weary face at the door. "Ma'am, I have a flat tire, and my phone is dead. By any chance, do you know how to..."

Yes. I do. And of course. You're here. They find me. They always do.

"Why?"

"She's pregnant."

"The cat is pregnant? And you kicked her out?"

Pause.

Daddy placed his newspaper down in his lap, leaned forward, looked me straight in the eye, and said, "Yes. And I'll do the same to you."

Alrighty then!

Daddy's other favorite pastime was scaring boys who came to take me out on dates. His favorite question to ask them was, naturally, "How's your sex life?"

I wish I could say that I had grown immune to Daddy's antics, but instead, his ludicrous icebreakers amused me. Watching boys stammer and respond with "Um, non-existent, sir?" brought me and Daddy endless laughs. The icing on the cake was his crazy-eyed look and stone-cold killer retort: "That's right. Not with my daughter."

I didn't really have a lot of second dates in high school.

When he wasn't ruining my social life, Daddy spent his afternoons at the local library. Daddy's appetite for reading was nothing short of voracious. He'd consume a 500-page book on world history in the course of a few hours and be ready to discuss it, point and counterpoint, with anyone willing to listen.

Since his audience was slim, Daddy resorted to telling tales with dramatic flair in order to get our attention. My personal favorite was his summary of Woodstock:

"Those dirty, crazy hippies were an embarrassment to this country! And their music was awful! All that free love and shit! You know what free love gets you? THE CLAP! And those women oughta put on bras and get home and cook something. Everybody there needed a shower!"

What we all needed was a Valium drip.

Eventually, Daddy would cease storytelling and take up his

other favorite pastime, beer drinking, and soon enough, he'd pass out, and the rest of us would celebrate the end of our collective dinnertime misery.

Daddy has been gone for decades, but his signature contribution to family tradition lives on: The "Bill H. Phenomenon."

For reasons no one really knows, Daddy always signed cards to my mother "Love, Your Husband, Bill H."

That's right, folks. The man who grew up alongside my mother in the same neighborhood, who dated my mother for 20 YEARS before finally marrying her, felt a primal need to clarify his relationship with her not only by reminding her of their relationship to one another but by also adding his surname initial.

Yet to the Harrington Clan, signing a card this way was "just another Tuesday." None of the family found it strange. (Well, maybe my mother did, but she didn't say much about it.)

Then along came me and my thankless role as the person who pointed out the weirdness in my family.

I was about 16, hanging out with my friend Stacy at her house when she showed me a romantic card her dad bought for her mom on Valentine's Day.

For teens, placing "romance" and "parents" together seemed odd, if not downright bizarre. But the card was beautiful. It had flowers on it and "For My Wife" emblazoned on it in fancy cursive writing. Inside was a lovely verse proclaiming souls melding into one or some such.

While we looked at the card, agog at the details and the outright romantic gesture it symbolized, something else caught my eye.

Stacy's dad signed the card, "Love, Don."

Not, "Love, your husband, Don B." Simply, "Love, Don."

Suddenly, I realized how bizarre it was that my father was identifying himself to HIS OWN WIFE on a card. Why was he doing this? Was my mom married before? Even if she was, she wasn't a polygamist! WHY THE HELL WAS HE SIGNING CARDS LIKE THIS??!?!

I kept this question to myself until I got home that night when I made the mistake of bringing up the matter at the dinner table.

"Daddy, why do you sign your cards to Mom with your last initial?"

"What?"

"When you sign cards to mom, you sign them, 'Love, Your Husband, Bill H.'"

"WHAT, ARE YOU JEALOUS?!?!?! FINE! I will sign your cards that way too! JESUS, MARY, AND JOSEPH, no one is ever happy around here!"

"Billy, you have to admit, it is a little strange," my mother said.

"I don't have to admit diddly! You people are UNBELIEVABLE!"

So from there on in, Daddy signed everything to us "Love, Your Father, Bill H." And complained about it. Every. Single. Time.

Bill H. has been gone for more than 30 years, yet this tradition continues. My brother is in my phone as "My Brother Charlie H.," and we all sign cards to each other "Love, Your Daughter, Judi H." or "Your Sister, Judi H.," "Your Mother, Mary H." "Your Son, Charlie H.," etc.

And in the ultimate honoring of the man who brought us so much craziness, my kids refer to their grandfather as "Grandpa Bill H."

"Much else" had arrived.

Dialing the phone, he motioned to us, saying, "Turn down the radio; I don't want interference."

All of a sudden, the guy who loathed modern technology wanted to be Walter Cronkite.

"What do you think he's going to say?" I asked.

"I don't know, but I bet we are going to remember it the rest of our lives," said my mother.

"Yeah, hello? Yeah, this is God."

Boy, was my mother right.

"Yes, you heard me! This is GOD! I am calling tonight because I want you to know that the Yankees are NOT MY DAMN BASE-BALL TEAM, you crazy kook!"

Pot, meet kettle.

"No, the BOSTON RED SOX ARE GOD'S BASEBALL TEAM, YOU HERETIC!!!!"

At this point, my mother ran to the bathroom because she was laughing so hard. My brother went to the fridge to get some ice cream. I asked him to get me a bowl. This show was getting great.

"I want to reward THE FAITHFUL, not the DAMN YANKEES!"

Bill H. looked over at us, pointing to the phone, nodding his head maniacally as if to say, "Yeah, I got them REAL GOOD!" We just sat there, shoveling ice cream in our mouths.

Then, just when we thought it couldn't get any crazier, Bill H. said, "This isn't the last you'll hear from ME! I'LL CALL AGAIN!"

Thank you for warning us all.

Bill H. became a regular call-in personality. Every time he decided he'd call, he'd look at all of us, place his finger to his lips and say, "Now keep this between us, okay?"

Oh, don't worry, we aren't exactly running around bragging about your literal God complex. Your secret is safe here!

Finally, after a few weeks of this nonsense, it occurred to me that maybe I had some bragging rights here too.

"Daddy, if you are telling them you are God, does this make me the Daughter of God?"

"Don't be a smartass!"

He's impersonating the Father Almighty, and I'm a smartass? Classic Bill H. He was an original. The Original Mass-hole.

My Mother, Mary H.

Like Bill H., my mother, Mary H., has a signature story. Hers involves dressing as The Cat in the Hat.

You know, like one does.

Before you think my mother is a fetishist of epic proportions, let me assure you: There is a perfectly reasonable explanation for her sartorial choices.

When my mom entered retirement, she took a part-time job as a reading assistant in the public school system. She spent most of her time with kindergarteners and first graders, particularly kids who struggled with reading. She seemed to have a knack for engaging these kids, so that was where the teachers let her focus.

I am certain my mother took this job to justify reading children's literature while waiting for her kids (meaning "me") to make her a grandmother. My reason for thinking so? Her devotion to reading Dr. Seuss books. My mother has always loved Dr. Seuss. I still have my copy of *To Think That They Saw It On Mulberry Street*, which she and I read together hundreds of times.

If you have children in school, you know that Dr. Seuss is a literary deity to whom teachers pay homage every year on his birthday, March 2.

Do you see where this is going?

Yes, the first year my mom worked in the school system, someone came up with the great idea that she should dress as The Cat in the Hat for Dr. Seuss's birthday. And she didn't argue. She just did it because "it made the kids happy!"

A star was born.

From that day forward, my mother dressed up as The Cat in

the Hat each year on Dr. Seuss's birthday. She even walked to work once in her costume, tail and everything. She didn't care. Clearly, no one else did either, least of all the local police. She was on local cable TV once, which launched her into Fall River celebrity status. Given that Fall River's most famous citizen is the alleged ax murderer, Lizzie Borden, I suppose this was a welcome public relations move for the city.

Word got out in the school community that she was greeting trick-or-treaters dressed as The Cat in the Hat, and students who hadn't seen her in years would show up just to visit with her and reminisce about when she was The Cat in the Hat for THEIR classroom.

As for how our family reacted to this newly found hobby of my mother's, let's suffice to say it took on a life of its own; and by that, I mean "we were all fully entrenched in Stockholm Syndrome and no longer found this unusual."

Case in point: I had a picture of my mom on my office desk, and when people asked me who it was, I simply said, "Oh yeah, my mom dresses like The Cat in the Hat" and carried on, business as usual. Thankfully, I had friends who knew there had to be a larger story and were kind enough to ask it without inquiring if my mother perhaps lived in an institution.

Once I told the story, people understood. We all started referring to my mother, Mary H., by a new nickname: The Cat.

When I found out I was pregnant with Ruth, people began taking bets as to whether my mother would show up at the hospital dressed as The Cat in the Hat. I quickly put the kibosh on that scheme by reiterating my policy regarding birth: I barely wanted to be in the room; I sure as hell wasn't inviting my mother, costume or no costume.

After Ruth was born, my mother's "Nana job" was to read books by our family's favorite author to her beloved grandchild. And because our family is a living testament to the adage "go big or

The Mysterious Mr. Soup

The next stop on this runaway train through Dysfunction Junction involves a clandestine romance between two senior citizens.

The damsel in this tale of wonder (as in "what wondrous fuckery is this?") involves none other than My Mother Mary H., who we learned from previous episodes was dubbed Nana Cat for her love of Dr. Seuss.

Around the same time as Nana Cat's ordination, she simultaneously morphed into a cougar. She started dating a gentleman named Don, who, depending on who you asked, was anywhere between 5 and 10 years her junior.

Cougar status is a long-standing tradition in our family. Both of my grandmothers took on younger male companions in their later years. In the case of my paternal grandmother, Betty H. (yes, she signed her cards that way too), her companion, Frank, was 15 years younger. Some people think the idea of a cougar is controversial; in our family, we just call it Tuesday.

I can't speak for how my grandmothers met their beaus (and knowing our family, I'd rather live in ignorance), but in the case of Nana Cat and Don, they met as volunteers in the Fall River school system, with Nana Cat reading to elementary school children a couple of times a week and Don chauffeuring my mother and a gaggle of other grannies to and from their respective schools a couple of times a week.

And was Don attracted to Nana's sparkling personality, spirit of community service, or (I fear) her furry cat costume complete with a swishing tail? We will never know and thank Jesus and all the angels and saints for that.

My mother would tell me tales of all the schoolgirl chatter on the bus and how Don, the token male, would joke alongside them all. Over time, they all began to refer to the van as The Blue-Haired Bus, a reference to the bluish-tinted hair of all the minivan's female inhabitants, or, as they called themselves, The Granny Posse.

Over time, my mother began to refer to Don as "her friend."

I took note and remained quiet, waiting for the day she'd announce they were dating.

Of course, my patience was also an act of denial. By the time my mother met Don, I was in my mid-thirties, and the thought of my mother dating was, well, weird. She'd been widowed for nearly two decades. I'd made the mistake once of telling her that I didn't mind if she wanted to date, which was met with the fiery response, "I spent 18 years waiting for my freedom from your father. I'm in no hurry to lose it again."

So in the ultimate role reversal, I found myself both eagerly anticipating and cautiously dreading what seemed to be my mother's inevitable rite of passage.

Finally, the day came.

In classic Mary H. fashion, she coyly asked me, "Do I still have your permission to date?"

"Since when do you need permission to do anything?"

"Well, I thought I'd ask since I have a date tonight."

"With a man?"

"YES, WITH A MAN!"

"Well, Ma, late-life lesbianism is real, so I thought I'd ask. But of course, I know you have a date with Don."

"HOW DID YOU KNOW THAT?!!?!"

"You talk about him all the time, Ma. I'm happy for you. I want you to go out and have fun."

And so it began. My mother and Don began dining together a couple of times a week. Sometimes they'd go out, and sometimes she'd cook for them at her apartment. A big night out would involve the preferred gambling method of the Catholic Church, BINGO.

As Nana Cat and Don's relationship progressed, my family grew. Ruth was a toddler when Don arrived on the scene, and Zoe arrived a few months later.

My mother continued her weekly pilgrimage to see her grandchildren, and I'd hear about her latest excursions with Don—their drives to get ice cream and their shared love of the Boston Red Sox.

Likewise, Don heard about Ruth and Zoe and their antics as babies and toddlers, especially the nickname we had come up with for him, Mr. Soup.

Calling Don "Mr. Soup" was born out of necessity. Perplexed upon learning that Nana Cat was not going to visit as scheduled one afternoon, three-year-old Ruth waged a campaign akin to a Freedom of Information Act request, demanding to know why Nana Cat had to cancel plans.

"Why is Nana Cat not coming to play with us?"

"Nana Cat has dinner plans with a friend. She will come up another time."

"Who is her friend?" Ruth asked.

"Um, I'm not sure."

"What's her friend's name?"

"Not sure."

"Tell me."

What to do? How to explain that Nana had a boyfriend? That term was weird enough, given they were in their sixties and seventies. "Boyfriend" and "girlfriend" to me are terms for teenagers, not senior citizens.

And while I was genuinely happy for Nana Cat and harbored zero resentment toward Don, the thought of referring to him as "Grandpa," thrusting a role on a man I had yet to meet and who had no kids (that he knew of) felt at best presumptuous; at worst, downright deceptive.

I didn't want the girls to think they had a grandpa if his relationship with my mother were to be short-lived. It was bad enough I was going to have to explain Santa and the Easter Bunny to the kids at some point; I wasn't about to un-tell the telling of Don.

Finally, I remembered that my mom told me that Don likes soup, so I came up with the most logical option.

"His name is Mr. Soup."

"Mr. Soup? Why is he Mr. Soup?"

"Because Nana makes soup for him."

"Oh, okay."

Right around the time we christened Don "Mr. Soup," I came to the realization that we had yet to meet Don.

Did Mr. Soup even exist?

In a reprise of my role as the family inquisitor, I began to drop hints that we might want to meet the man my mother had been dating for (at this point) two years.

"So, Ma, what's Don doing for Thanksgiving? Would he like to join us?"

"Oh, no, thanks, honey. He goes to his nephew's house."

"Well, we don't have to wait for a holiday for Don to join us for a meal. Maybe he can visit with you next time you come up?"

"Oh, he's busy."

Reasoning that very few of my boyfriends ever crossed my mother's threshold, I left the topic alone.

Until I heard that my brother, who was still living in Japan but had come home for a visit, had met Don.

As is typical in our family, I didn't hear about the two of them meeting until after my brother returned to Osaka.

"How come Charlie got to meet Don?" I asked.

My mother clearly took offense at this most ludicrous of questions.

"Well, Charlie was here at my house, and Don came here for dinner!" she reasoned.

"But you and Charlie drove up to my house to visit. Why couldn't Don come along?"

"He was busy."

"Not too busy to hang out with Charlie!"

"Well, Charlie was here from a foreign country."

"I have to move to Japan to meet someone who lives an hour away from me and has been dating my mother for two years?"

"I don't know why you're offended. It was just a matter of timing."

Of course, my mother was harboring Mr. Soup like a fugitive, but I'm the unreasonable one.

I suggested changing Don's name from Mr. Soup to George Glass in honor of Jan Brady's imaginary boyfriend on *The Brady Bunch*.

"You need to let this go," my mother said.

So I did because I knew my silence would prompt a confession.

A few weeks later, apropos of absolutely nothing, my mother sheepishly admitted, "I'm afraid of what you're going to say to Don."

"What could I possibly say? 'Hi, welcome to our home; what can I get you to drink?' Really?"

Finally, it hit me.

Mary H. and Mr. Soup began dating in 2004, the year the Red Sox won the World Series.

To boot, Mary H. confessed to me that her first date with Don was on September 18, the same date as her first date with my father, Bill H., which was held at Fenway Park.

I surmised that Mary H., while of course thrilled to see The Curse of the Bambino reversed, felt a guilt like no other on earth.

Not because she found happiness in widowhood, mind you. She had committed a greater sin; she shared in Bill H.'s lifelong dream—a Red Sox World Series win—with another man.

Therefore, it is completely reasonable to presume that I, as Bill

H.'s right-hand girl and fellow Red Sox nut, would remind her of this in front of her (new) beloved.

Mary H., of course, denied feeling so much as a morsel of guilt, citing that she waited 18 years after Bill H.'s death to start dating, and her stock excuse became, "What the hell is wrong with you and why can't you ever let this go? I just want to keep my life private, and not bringing Don to see you has nothing to do with the Red Sox winning the Series!"

I was ready to die upon this hill, or, rather, this baseball mound, and continued to serve as Our Lady of Perpetual Hell, insisting that my mother was hiding Mr. Soup in shame because she saw the Red Sox win WITH HIM.

Did I really feel this way? I will neither confirm nor deny my feelings, except to say that I was Daddy's girl, Freudian nightmares run deep, and the Red Sox Nation runs deeper.

Then the tide changed. I finally met Mr. Soup.

I wish I could say my mother introduced us voluntarily, but I think we can all agree that the answer to that is "of course not." I met him when Mary H. was in a rehabilitation facility following an acute cardiac event that required a pacemaker.

This is what it took, folks—a life-threatening medical event.

Fuckery knows no bounds with the Harrington Clan.

When Mary H. was in the hospital, it was touch-and-go. While I waited for Charlie to fly in from Japan, I asked a priest to administer Anointing of the Sick (or what many know as "Last Rites"), and I made sure that Mr. Soup was on the approved visitor list. While we didn't cross paths in the hospital, I was assured he visited my mother every day.

Not ready to leave this world yet, Mary H. rallied, and within a week, she was transferred to rehab, where she returned to torturing us (and by "us," I mean "me") in new and exciting ways.

"My room is next to the cemetery. You know what that means," she said bitterly, implying that her room location was a harbinger of death, to be ushered in by a tribe of Nurse Ratcheds and a special guest appearance of Kathy Bates' character from the movie *Misery*, based on the Stephen King novel.

"It means you have quiet neighbors, Ma," I replied with resignation.

"You're going to leave me here."

"Don't tempt me," I replied.

And so it went for a few weeks until, by fate, I arrived with six-year-old Ruth at the same time Mr. Soup showed up.

A large man with a kind face and quiet demeanor, Don strolled in and greeted us as if he'd known us all our lives.

"Hi, I'm Don, or as you might know me, Ruthie, Mr. Soup."

Ruth, a reticent child by nature, was agog at the prospect that Mr. Soup existed. She stared as if witnessing Santa Claus, the Easter Bunny, and the Tooth Fairly all at once.

While Ruth's response was typical, Mary H.'s was not. Starry-eyed and wistful, her wide, toothy smile upon seeing Don was nothing short of miraculous. Her shoulders sagged down as her tension eased, as she smiled demurely when Don gave her a peck on the cheek.

I found myself resisting the temptation to search for a pod under the bed or other signs of alien abduction. Instead, I released my own tension about my mother's beau, genuinely happy that this chapter of life was bringing her so much joy.

That day at Mom's bedside marked the beginning of Don's presence in our lives, which continued for several years, spanning birthdays and holidays. Each time I saw my mom and Mr. Soup together, I felt this pang that I can only describe as something akin to watching your child venture out on their first date; you're happy and sad all at once.

But with Mary H., there was the added dimension of relief. Her marriage to Bill H. was fraught with frustration at best, trauma at worst. Such is life alongside a raging alcoholic whose unpredictable anger seemed limitless. To be able to trust herself to love someone else again must have been hard, but she took the chance and trusted her gut, and found a companion in her later years.

Raising parents is hard work, but the rewards are worth it.

My Brother, Charlie H.

Every Major League Baseball player has what is called a "Walk-up Song," an anthem played in the stadium as the player is walking from the on-deck circle and getting ready to bat. For example, when David "Big Papi" Ortiz sauntered up to home plate, The Notorious B.I.G.'s "Big Poppa" blasted throughout Fenway Park.

My brother, Charlie H., and I have "walk-up phrases." Mine is "putting the 'fun' in 'dysfunctional' since 1969." His is "the best jokes never die."

For Charlie H., his walk-up phrase is more of a personal mantra, one he lives by and invokes at every opportunity.

When I was toiling away at my first job after college in the early 1990s, I called him from work and asked him to leave me a reminder to bring a dress to work for my friend, Amanda, to borrow. I came home that evening to find approximately 5,000 sticky notes all over our house with "Don't forget the dress!" scrawled on them. They were on my bedroom door, the refrigerator, the milk inside the refrigerator, the bathroom, the toilet tank, the bathroom mirror, the television set, you get the idea. Twenty-five years later, he periodically haunts me by Facebook or text with "Don't forget the dress!"

As a devoted fan of the author Ian Fleming and Fleming's most famous character, James Bond, Charlie fancies himself an International Man of Mystery (IMOM), a one-man/one-fan show he took on the road in 1998 when he moved to Japan for the professional pursuit of teaching English to Japanese businessmen, the virtuous pursuits of photography and hiking, and the personal pursuits of debauchery and women.

Given that Charlie's time in Japan preceded iPhone photo days, he took to sending photos of his adventures to us, and by "us," I mean "our dear mother, Mary H." One particular photo portrays Charlie in the company of four women, all of them having a great time on their way to or from an epic rager. Charlie's arms drape the shoulders of the two in the middle, and his expression—wide-eyed, big smile, like "Hi, Ma! Look at me!"—embodies the phrase "a picture speaks a thousand words."

My mother's words were, "Well, look! Charlie is making friends!"

My words were less generous. "Well, I know what I'm sending him for Christmas: condoms."

Charlie did eventually settle down for a while with a woman named Sayaka, and while they opted out of having a human family, they were pet parents to a bunny named Peter. When Peter met his maker, Sayaka took it very hard and, unbeknownst to Charlie, scoured the internet for a temple that performed pet funerals. Early one morning, Charlie woke up to find a Buddhist priest at the front door, with a mobile crematorium parked out front, a true embodiment of his and Sayaka's cultural differences.

Charlie's IMOM tour ended in 2011, on the heels of the Fukushima Daiichi nuclear disaster. He returned home to Massachusetts when the girls were in grade school. Sayaka did not return with him. She remained in Japan to care for her elderly mother, a heartache Charlie and I have spoken of only once but remains seared on my memory as one of the few times he wore his heart on his sleeve.

We all cope with loss and grief in our own ways. After the end of an important relationship, some people retreat into their hermit cave to lick their wounds in solitude. Some sob into a pint of ice cream. Some get angry and cynical. My brother's coping mechanism was humor. He dedicated himself to being the family's court jester and dove into this role with relentless commitment, more so than ever before. He seemed determined to fill our

"I heard the girls got great report cards...will you be celebrating by opening the pool?"

"Happy St. Patrick's Day! Will the pool water be tinted green this year?"

"Happy Easter! Can I wear a bunny suit to the opening of the pool today?"

But the real character in all this poolside fuckery is a character whom we like to think of as Charlie's alter ego, an homage to his adventures in Asia that simultaneously infuses Charlie's perception of himself as Playboy of the Western (meets Eastern) World.

Everyone, meet Quan. Or, as my brother calls him, "Quan, My Friend in the Chinese Mafia."

Seldom seen, often referenced, and sometimes heard from, Quan from the Chinese Mafia ("Quan" for short) is a mischievous character who fancies himself a filmmaker, forever in hot pursuit of a film set to produce a series of films within the LEGO genre.

"A Very LEGO Jaws"

"A Very LEGO 2016 Summer Olympics"

"A Very LEGO Baseball Season"

"A Very LEGO Titanic"

"A Very LEGO Barbershop Quartet"

As if the LEGO theme weren't curious enough, each film in this genre involves a requisite water scene, whether or not it's obvious from the title.

Which, of course, means that Quan calls me when I least expect it to ask me to host him and his mighty film crew at—you guessed it!—MY POOL!

That's right! Quan does not travel solo. He's typically accompanied by an entourage of strippers and henchmen, all of who exclusively drink top-shelf liquor. I have informed Quan he will need to BYOB and C (condoms), and any children sired on set will not be taken in by my real family.

For a long time, Quan's gender was presumed female (by me),

but it turns out Quan is meant to sound like George Takei of Star Trek fame, according to my brother.

There are so many problems with this assertion; I scarcely know where to begin. For one thing, Mr. Takei was born in Los Angeles and is of Japanese ancestry, and has literally nothing to do with either China or the mafia. But try explaining this to my brother, and he'll just ask, "So anyway, is the pool open yet?"

There is also the problem that while I know that Quan is imaginary, I seem to be alone in this assessment. Thanks to the Poolside Peanut Gallery made up of Charlie's derelict friends (and okay, some of the degenerates in my life), I'm asked "Is the pool open?" and "Where's Quan?" as often as possible, both on social media and in real life.

Quan has taken on a life of his own amongst my friends, and it continually amazes me how many people suspend all disbelief when they learn of him. For instance, I was with my friends Nikki and Renee, and when Quan's name came up, Renee asked who he was.

"Judi's brother's friend in the Chinese mafia," Nikki said matter-of-factly.

Cigarette in hand, Renee simply replied, "Oh, okay," shrugged her shoulders, and lit up.

In 2018, we took the pool down, reasoning that the pool liner resembled a patchwork quilt, the siding had rusted, and we hadn't opened it in two years.

I was smug in this development, thinking that I would have the last laugh, having won the pool war of the early 2000s. In particular, I was reveling in the thought that I would be further spared the antics of Quan, My Brother's Friend in the Chinese Mafia, his band of hookers, and Quan's degenerate film crew, and could gain at least a modicum of peace in my life.

Mick and the girls tore down the pool on April 1, 2018, which happened to also be Easter Sunday. Incapable of passing up an opportunity to uphold my reputation as The Worst Catholic Ever, I posted pictures of the pool's demise on Facebook with the caption:

Christ is risen, and the pool is coming down!

The post incited a riot, but not of a religious kind. Instead, people began commenting:

"What about Quan?"

"What is Quan going to do?"

"How can you do this to Quan?"

My phone began to blow up with texts, phone calls, emails, asking the $64,000 question: What about Quan? I fully expected someone to show up with an Edible Arrangement offering their sympathy for Quan's loss. In one case, someone threatened to coordinate a protest outside our house.

Thank Jesus (quite literally), neither of those things happened.

Quan has since faded into oblivion (again, thank you, Lord), but his memory lives on in mysteriously timed phone calls or texts from Charlie asking me if he and Quan can film at the "Location Formerly Known as The Pool."

We've since moved. Looks like Quan's career is over.

That being said, with my brother? You never know. I might install a hot tub next year, which means that Quan (or a brand-new imaginary friend) might arrive. I am already bracing myself. God help us all.

Trailer Park Dreams

As the treasured "miracle child" of Bill H. and The Cat, my first birthday was a big to-do for the whole family.

Bill H. and The Cat were in their mid-to-late-thirties when they got married, and my arrival was deemed miraculous because doctors told The Cat she couldn't have children. I am not sure if this was just doctors shaming a thirty-something woman or if there was a legitimate reason for this diagnosis.

Regardless, if you know The Cat, you know that none of us will ever find out because the mythology has been set in stone: She was barren, and suddenly two days before I was born, she was told she was pregnant. Yes, TWO DAYS. How doctors miss an eight-pound baby is beyond me, but this was 1969, and perhaps everyone was too busy drinking martinis to notice.

My "miraculous" status was enhanced by the fact that I was allegedly the first girl on the Harrington side of the family in several generations (also a myth, according to ancestry.com, but why let facts get in the way of a good story). As such, Bill H.'s brothers were completely smitten with me from the moment I arrived on the planet.

And that is how it came to pass that when my first birthday rolled around, my parents hosted the typical Beer and Birthday Cake party so common in the 1970s. Note the priority.

As is typical in a family with questionable standards, the party came complete with an epic drama, which in our case involved The Dress From Hell.

The tale begins with my Uncle Eddie's wife, Dottie, who probably invented the term "pre-gaming:" I do not recall a single story where she wasn't described by the level of her drunken stupor.

Dottie had been placed in charge by Eddie of getting me "a nice birthday dress," and it seems that got mistaken for "a nice bottle of Scotch and maybe something for the baby."

According to The Cat, when it came time to open gifts, Eddie was insistent on his and Dottie's being opened first. My mother obliged and discovered what was likely a dress from a used clothing store that probably needed to be ironed, but, according to my mother, "looked like it had been dragged through the mud and someone shit on it." In every telling of this tale, the description of the dress gets worse. "It was eaten by moths." "It was shredded into ribbons." "There was a baggy of cocaine in one pocket." With each retelling of the story, the descriptions escalated. The way my mother described it, you would think this birthday dress had been pulled directly from the bottom of a wet garbage bag on a humid summer day.

At any rate, you get the point: It wasn't the nice dress Eddie had envisioned, and my mother quickly had to divert attention from it so that Eddie could save face, and the family could save themselves from pooling bail money for him and put those funds toward a run to the packie to get more booze.

Eddie and Dottie split up not long after The Dottie and The Dress Incident. And by that, I mean "They went to a wedding, Dottie passed out drunk, then Eddie packed his bags and left her on the couch. For 10 years."

I learned of all of these shenanigans when I was about seven, and we were visiting with Bill H.'s mom, Betty H. (she signed her cards that way too), and she would weep and wail for Eddie. I thought he was dead, but my mother had to finally tell me what was going on, which was how I learned about Dottie and The Dress.

I also learned that Betty H., despite what she had told the police, knew exactly where Eddie was and wasn't going to tell anyone. Several times a year, she would get flowers from Eddie, and each time she would say, "This is all because of that no good Dottie! I just wish she would drop dead so I can see my boy again!"

Well, as they say in Disney, "A dream is a wish your heart makes," and soon enough, Betty H.'s wish came true, and Dottie died. Approximately three hours after her demise, Eddie's previously undisclosed location was revealed. He was living in Vegas and worked at a casino. Betty H. told us he was a croupier, but knowing our family, he was probably a bartender.

A few months later, Eddie came to visit. The Cat announced his impending arrival to me and my brother, Charlie, with a tone reserved for inside secrets, except Charlie had no idea what the hell she was talking about.

Which led The Cat to regale us all with the story no one asked her to tell: Dottie and The Dirty Dress. In this rendition, the dress "appeared to have been buried and dug back up again."

Charlie's only question was whether Eddie knew any hookers and exotic dancers from his life in Vegas.

"Where did you learn such things!?!" asked The Cat.

"Clearly, he overheard Daddy asking the same thing!" I said.

When I arrived home from school a few days later, Eddie was sitting in our living room with Bill H., where they were smoking and drinking beers. Yes, at 4 p.m. If there was ever a question as to whether this man was really my uncle, that scene sealed the deal that he was.

Eddie had brought some pictures with him from ~~life on the lam~~ his life in Vegas. I am not entirely sure what I was expecting to see when he opened the photo album, but I can assure you a double-wide trailer was not one of them.

"This is where I live!" Eddie proclaimed.

I literally have no idea to this day what other pictures Eddie displayed because the picture of that double-wide trailer is branded on my memory like Sharpie marker on a white couch.

"Oh, that looks so cool!" I replied, eyes widened, mouth agog.

I was enthralled. It looked like such a fun way to live, so compact and efficient (to this day, I am obsessed with well-used space, particularly if it is small). I was already intrigued with the woman on the show *Real People* who drove a semi and lived in the cab of her truck, so in my mind, living in a trailer was a serious upgrade.

Eddie's visit lasted a few days, and he returned to Vegas, bringing Betty H. with him. I bet my mother had wished she had fed Dottie arsenic-laced turkey at Thanksgiving a few years earlier; she was so happy to see Betty H. leave.

I continued to dream of the trailer park Eddie lived in. Did they have a garden? Did he host BBQs with his neighbors? The possibilities seemed endless to me.

In a moment of unfettered enthusiasm (and naivete), I decided that I shouldn't keep my dreams to myself; I should try to bring them to life by sharing them with my family. Dinnertime seemed the most appropriate setting to announce what I thought would be a great adventure in family bonding.

"Do you guys think we could move to a trailer park?"

Silence.

Bill H. put out his cigarette, slammed his hands on the table, and bellowed, "JESUS H. CHRIST! Are you out of your ever-loving MIND?!??!!"

"No, Daddy, I saw Uncle Eddie's pictures, and I thought it looked like fun! It would be like camping all the time!"

"Mary, did you put her up to this?"

"No, Billy, she came up with this one all on her own."

My brother piped in with, "She shouldn't be left alone, it looks like."

Bill H. continued his rant, "FOR THE LOVE OF PETE, I was mortified to see my brother living in a trailer park, and now this one wants us all to move into one? And CAMPING?!?! We haven't camped a day in our lives!"

"We could start!" I said—the hope-filled child that I was.

"It is NOT happening. We are staying right here where we are."

Undeterred, I decided to take my dreams to the Lord. The Cat had instilled in us a strong belief in prayer, so I figured no better place to practice what she preached than at Sunday Mass, during the Prayers of the Faithful, no less.

When the priest asked us to take a moment to pray for our own intentions, I prayed in my Best Irish Whisper, "Dear Lord, please let us move to the trailer park!"

My mother, horrified, responded (perhaps a little too loudly), "Judith Marie Harrington, you stop praying right now."

So from there on in, I kept my little dream to myself. But true to the adage "Your dreams are answered when you least expect it" I found my trailer park dream in the most unlikely place:

Donegal, Ireland.

Yes, folks, there is a trailer park just down the road from my in-laws! Of course, they insist on calling it the "caravan park" to make it sound classier—potato, potah-to (see what I did there?). I remain hopeful that someday, in my twilight years, I will get to spend at least a summer in one of those little caravans (except I will call it My Trailer of Hope).

And I will think of Uncle Eddie. And maybe I will dig a festive birthday dress out of the garbage bin and wear it proudly, in his (and dear Aunt Dottie's) honor.

"There's no air conditioning in your apartment. It must get hot when you cook all the time for me."

Or a television set.

"Yours has lousy reception, and this one has a VCR built in, so we can watch movies."

Or a stereo.

"Your little clock radio has seen better days."

And you know they are serious if, on your first dating anniversary, you get a vacuum cleaner.

Romantic? No. Practical? Yes.

Years later, he told me, "I knew we needed all those things, so I just got them."

Romance isn't always what you've been taught. It's something you learn.

Lost in Translation: Irish-Style

If there ever were a phrase that summed up my marriage perfectly, it would be "lost in translation." The irony of this motto is that, from all appearances, everyone in my family speaks English as their primary language. However, because my husband is from Ireland, we are more of a house divided by a common language.

The earliest example of our signature linguistic phenomenon is an incident we lovingly refer to as "Wee Beastie." It took place when we were newlyweds and had moved from our apartment into our first single-family home together.

I arrived at the breakfast table one morning to find Mick making tea and toast.

"Good morning."

"We have a wee beastie."

"And there's a morning announcement I didn't expect. Do you mean a skunk?"

"No, the other kind."

"An opossum?"

"Nope."

"Am I supposed to keep guessing?"

"If you want."

"Where did you see it?"

"Outside. It comes up from underneath the sunroom porch and walks around the yard and then walks down the driveway at 5:25 a.m."

"You're timing it?"

"Yes."

"Do you two chat or something?"

"No. I'm going to work now."

I didn't think about our backyard critter much until a few weeks later; while I was on the phone with my mother, Mick started yelling, "THE WEE BEASTIE IS HERE!!!!"

The Cat, true to form as the inspiring force behind the phrase "making a mountain out of a molehill," panicked. Given Mick's tendency to speak barely above a whisper, she felt it was akin to a Category 4 hurricane.

"Judi, what is the matter?" she screamed into the phone.

"Nothing. Mick is yelling about the backyard vermin."

"You should go help him!"

"Yes, because my six-foot-three-inch husband, who is built like a linebacker, may perish at the sight of what is most likely a skunk or raccoon."

"I knew that neighborhood was not for you."

"Goodbye, Ma."

So I head to the porch, where Mick is standing pointing at this alleged "Beastie" and discover that it is, in fact, AS I HAD SUS-PECTED AND CLEARLY STATED, a skunk.

A very pregnant skunk.

"Judi, see? It's a wee beastie!"

"That is a skunk."

"It is?"

One of the most frustrating attributes of Mick's communica-tion style (and what I have learned is generally the style of Don-egal men) is that they will ask you a question and then question the answer.

I took a few deep breaths and replied, "Yes, it is a skunk."

Nothing in life could have prepared me for what Mick was about to say next.

"It doesn't look like Pepe LePew."

Silence.

Finally, after several (more) deep breaths, I asked, as calmly as possible, "Are you telling me that your entire frame of reference for urban wildlife is *Looney Tunes*?"

"Yes. Are you sure that's a skunk because Pepe Le Pew's stripe starts lower on his nose than that Wee Beastie?"

"I am sure. Good night. I'm going to bed."

"It's 6 p.m."

"I am done with this day."

The Wee Beastie returned a few years later when we discovered that opossums were living under our backyard deck. One had met an untimely demise, having been hit by a car in front of the house, but one Sunday morning, Mick discovered one sitting out on the deck.

In true Mick fashion, he made the announcement the way one might say "cow!" when driving along the countryside.

"Wee Beastie on the back deck!"

"Do you mean a skunk?"

"No, the other kind."

"An opossum?"

"No."

Realizing Mick had no idea what an opossum looked like (I'm guessing that St. Patrick drove out more than just snakes from Ireland), I got up from the table and looked outside to see—you guessed it!—an opossum.

"That's an opossum."

"Are you sure?"

"Yes, I am sure. Given I've lived in the U.S. my whole life and once worked as a park ranger, can you please trust me on this one?"

"Okay. What do you think it's doing?"

"Nothing. It's an opossum. It's playing opossum."

"I don't know what that means."

"Opposums play dead. This guy may look like he's out there sunning himself, but he's really waiting to do something nasty."

"How do you know this?"

"We already covered that. Listen, opossums are nocturnal. He's out in broad daylight, which means he is likely rabid."

"Maybe he's just sad about his friend who died."

Silence.

"What?"

"You know, the dead one that I had to get rid of the other day. Maybe he just misses his friend."

"Yes, of course. Let's gather and pray alongside him."

"Do you want to?"

"NO, I DO NOT WANT TO GO OUTSIDE AND HOLD A PRAYER CIRCLE WITH AN OPOSSUM. I am eight months pregnant, and we need to get to Lamaze class, not for the sake of our unborn baby, but so that I can hone my breathings skills to deal with this nonsense."

I don't remember what happened to the opossum because not long after, our first child, Ruth, was born. But I'll always remember Mick's empathy for the opossum and all of nature's rich pageant that scampered across our yard, our deck, and our lives.

The Bitch Who Stole Christmas

When you ask most people about their most vivid Christmas memory, you are bound to hear a story of childhood and a long-wished-for toy or bauble or a Rockwellian image of exchanging gifts fireside with beloved grandparents.

In my case, my most memorable Christmas was the year I became known in our family as "The Bitch Who Stole Christmas."

The story is rooted in the tradition of the Harrington Family Manger, which was rumored to have been in our family for three generations. Of course, given my family's predilection for embellishment, it was more likely purchased out of the back of someone's truck in a seedy motel parking lot. Regardless of its origin, it is a very beautiful manger. The figurines are all hand-painted, and it comes complete with an angel to place on top of the manger itself.

True to form, the manger is not without its signature story. The manger is technically from The Cat's side of the house, the Johnson Clan. My grandmother Johnson, The Cat's mother (whose claim to fame was giving her nieces and nephews dimes inside prescription bottles), was the host of most Christmas gatherings of my mother's youth. Nana's brother, my uncle, John, was known for swapping the Black wise man with Joseph in a prank that annoyed my grandmother to no end. Nana couldn't conceive that Our Lord and Savior wasn't white.

He was definitely not the blonde, blue-eyed, long wavy haired hippie surfer white dude that he is often portrayed to be[1].

---

1   Historical records indicate that Jesus was most likely a "Palestinian Jewish man living in Galilee in the first century." (to quote History.com)

I know this.

My grandmother did not know this or simply could not accept this.

It is awkward to admit that my Nana and her brother were probably a little bit racist. Or maybe a lot racist. I don't know exactly what was going through his or her mind, but I presume it wasn't exactly "woke."

This situation epitomizes what it means to be a member of the Harrington-McLaughlin Family. We possess many terrific qualities. We are also pretty screwed up. Yet we never stop loving each other in spite of our many flaws and shortcomings. Whether it's racism or alcoholism, or even supporting a team other than the Red Sox (although that's a tough sell for some of us), we find a way to love one another despite our most unlovable qualities.

To be clear, I am not saying that racism is ever okay. I'm simply acknowledging the reality that Nana was born in 1904 and absorbed the horrific messages of that time, the culture she grew up in. In summary: Family is complicated.

After many years of admiring the manger, my mother passed it on to me to display in my first home after I married Mick.

At the same time, for completely unrelated reasons, my brother moved to Japan to take a job teaching English. Several years later, he came home for an extended stay while he sorted out some work visa issues. For a guy who is more akin to the Prodigal Son, my mother treated his return like the Second Coming of Christ.

Approximately seven minutes after his arrival, I received a phone call from my mother.

Me: "Hello?"

Mary H.: "Hi. I need the manger you took."

Me: "You mean the one you gave me?"

Mary H.: "Your brother is home for Christmas. They don't have Jesus there. They are BUDDHISTS, Judi!"

Me: "Well, Jesus is everywhere, they just don't recognize him, and did you notice it's Columbus Day weekend?"

Mary H.: "Well, I need that manger."

Me: "Come. And. Get. It."

For a woman in a big hurry, she waited until Thanksgiving to make the pilgrimage with Jesus Charlie Almighty to my house.

Me: "Happy Thanksgiving!"

Mary H.: "Where's the manger?"

Me: "Not on the menu."

I told my brother to grab the manger from the basement, where it was sitting on a table in a box marked "MANGER" in bold writing.

This did not happen. Why? Because God (and apparently, my own family) hates me.

The next day, I got a phone call from my mom.

Me: "Hello!"

Mary H.: "You still have the manger."

Me: "Because you didn't take it with you."

Mary H.: "Charlie says he couldn't find it."

Me: "Helen Keller could have found it."

Mary H.: "You must be hiding it."

Yes, folks, my mother believed that I was HIDING THE HOLY FAMILY!!! Perhaps I had Mary and Joseph tied up, back to back, duct tape over their mouths, and Jesus holding a ransom note. Who knows? I certainly do not. These people are more mysterious than The Holy Trinity.

Me: "It's here. You are welcome to come get it."

A week later, the Dynamic Duo arrived to take the hostages. The next morning—you guessed it!—I got a phone call.

Me: "Hello?"

Mary H.: "I have two Josephs."

Me: "What?!?!"

Mary H.: "I have two Josephs. Mary is not here. We can't have Christmas without Mary."

Me: "Actually, you can't have Christmas without Jesus."

Mary H.: "Where is Mary?"

By this time, I had reached my limit. I took a deep breath and replied:

"I thought this year we could have a little bit of fun with the manger. You see, the other man is Joseph's life partner, Bruce. On Christmas Day, there will be a big paternity reveal. Jerry Springer is officiating."

Mary H.: "That's not funny."

Me: "Mary is in there. Look again. I'll see you at Christmas."

And I took my phone off the hook.

EPILOGUE: (because everyone asks): The Virgin Mary and Mary H. were reunited once Mary H. completed unpacking the manger, where she discovered the Blessed Mother tucked in with the angel and a few farm animals. I have since regained custody of The Holy Family, following my brother Charlie H.'s return to Japan, where he continued to wander like a Jew in the desert, sometimes seeking Christ, but more likely chasing women.

Thus Sprach Our Jewish Kid.

On the face of it, our child asking for a menorah from Santa was funny all on its own. When the question of what Santa would bring came up, I told people the menorah story, and everyone had a chuckle. Some people couldn't believe Santa would bring the menorah, to which I invoked The Three Gifts Rule: If you ask Santa for three things, no matter what, Santa will do everything possible to bring them, even if one of them had nothing to do with Christmas.

The Three Gifts Rule was enacted by none other than My Father, Bill H. A Baptist by birth, Bill H. agreed to raise me and my brother in our mother's faith, Catholicism. While I would like to say that Daddy invoked The Three Gifts tradition out of love of Jesus and in the interest of keeping the holiday focused on Christ's birth, it is more likely a tradition born out of economic necessity. I also wish I could say that he gathered us in his lap and imparted the parameters of this rule in a gentle and loving way, but instead, he did it more like Archie Bunker. "Listen, it's three gifts around here. Good enough for Jesus, good enough for you. Make 'em good choices, but don't get crazy. Santa ain't made of money."

So, yes, a tradition started by a Baptist for his Catholic kids eventually led his grandchild to ask for an article of Judaica, which makes the story a little funnier. If only he were here to see it.

But what makes it the funniest of all is this: My husband is an Irish Catholic immigrant who was so determined to marry a woman of his own faith that he asked me on the first date if I was Catholic. (I am. I simply neglected to leave out the "recovering" part.)

And now our child wanted a menorah.

Based on her pronunciation, "venorah," I also wondered whether she was a Jewish gynecologist in a former life.

I decided to keep that second thought to myself, and after the girls went to bed, I broke the main news story to Mick.

"So, Ruthie wants Santa to bring her a menorah."

"What's a menorah?"

"It's used for Hanukkah, the Jewish holiday that comes around this time of year."

"How did she learn about Hanukkah?"

"I don't know. Must have been at school. Anyway, Santa is bringing it."

"Okay."

"It's probably a phase, and by Christmas, she won't even know what it is."

"Okay."

"I am pretty sure God is laughing right now."

"Probably."

"This is what you get for insisting on a Catholic wife."

"This is what you get for not being so Catholic."

"Probably."

Contrary to my prediction, Ruthie did not forget that Santa was bringing a menorah for Christmas. She also made sure that everyone in her midst knew about it. She told my mother. She told her teacher. She told the mailman. She told our hairdresser, Dolores. She told the pediatrician. She told our neighbors. And she told Santa at the mall. She announced it very matter-of-factly, "Santa is bringing me a menorah for Christmas," and continued on with her business of the moment.

Every announcement of what Santa was bringing prompted the same look on the listener's face: a gentle nodding, with a side-glance to me, who nodded in unison. I really didn't see much unusual about it. I knew Jews with Christmas trees. We were going to be Catholics with a menorah.

As promised, Santa brought the menorah to Ruthie. In fact, it was the first gift she opened on Christmas Day.

Every parent who celebrates Christmas with little ones tells you of the joy in watching their child's genuine belief in the magic surrounding Santa. But very few witness the joy of a little girl, with a menorah clutched to her chest, eyes closed, and head tilted to the sky, saying breathlessly, "Thank you, Santa, for my menorah."

I was happy to see my child embrace another culture, yet I felt a residual pang of guilt that somehow we were making a mockery of Judaism. Despite my Jewish friends telling me that Hanukkah is not a High Holy Day but rather a "light" holiday (no pun intended), I felt it important to pay a certain level of respect, and I set some rules around the menorah.

"Listen, you can play with the menorah until Christmas is over, but then it has to go up in the attic with the other holiday decorations. I do not want the menorah being broken out at Easter or the July 4 barbeque."

"Okay, Mama."

Ruthie and Zoe played with the menorah throughout winter break, I continued to consider the menorah a phase, and God laughed.

Ruthie returned to school after winter break, and on her first day back, I picked her up at the bus stop. As parents are wont to do, I asked about her day:

"Were you happy to see your friends?"

"Yes, especially Isabelle."

"Did the class talk about what Santa brought for presents or maybe what people got for Hanukkah?"

"Oh, we didn't talk about Hanukkah," she said as if speaking of it were a secret.

"Really? No one in your class celebrates Hanukkah?" I asked, peeking in the rearview mirror to see her response.

"Well, I do. I celebrate Hanukkah," she said as she pointed to herself and added, "But no one else does," in a tone that identified her as The Sole Jew in her kindergarten class. She quickly nodded her head as if to say, "Yep. That's it in a nutshell," and she said no more.

In Ruthie's world, she celebrated Hanukkah.

The Jewish theme continued throughout the remainder of kindergarten. It was mostly focused on Hanukkah because, in Ruthie's mind, that was The Only Jewish Holiday in the World. She continued to announce to anyone who would listen that Santa had brought her a menorah. The list grew to include her gastroenterologist (Ruthie lives with celiac disease and sees a GI specialist regularly), random cashiers at Target, and (my personal favorite) the woman she sat next to at a *Dora, Live!* production at the Colonial Theatre.

I dubbed her the spokesperson for Jews on the Move.

Once people learn of a theme in your home, they can't resist contributing to it. For instance, years ago, I had a collection of cow items: cookie jars, calendars, plates. As people learned of my affinity for cows, more cow-themed items appeared. A similar phenomenon began as word of the infamous Santa Brought Me a Menorah story spread amongst our family and friends: Judaica started to slowly but surely make its way into our abode.

Most of it came from our friends, the Collins Family, who, as native New Yorkers, are Jews by osmosis. Jacqueline sent a guide to Passover. Janet sent a Jewish calendar from the A&P. We hadn't started incorporating Passover and Yom Kippur into our lives, but Ruthie was thrilled to get mail, as all little kids are. I held my breath, knowing that with Hanukkah coming, there could only be more to come.

By Hanukkah 2009, I had given up all chance of Hanukkah as a fleeting phase. What sealed the deal was Ruthie's announcement at Thanksgiving that Hanukkah would start on December 11, quickly followed by the plea that we have "a Hanukkah party, with latkes."

Where she learned about latkes, I had no idea. Jewish traditions had seeped into our lives little by little, and I hadn't really fought against it, so it was plausible that somewhere along the line, latkes came up in conversation. Regardless, Ruthie had fixated on the notion of having fried shredded potatoes, and nothing else

Zoe and Her Imaginary Friends and Family and Fellow Inmates

Then there is Zoe, my delightful Zoe. The moment I heard the name, I immediately fell in love with it, specifically that it means "life" in Greek. I knew that if I had another daughter, her name would be Zoe.

I believe children are who they are from the moment of conception. Whereas Ruth was content to stay put in the womb and arrived two days past her due date, Zoe bounced around inside me like a pinball and arrived two weeks early with full-force screaming, as if to let the world know that she was here and would not go unnoticed.

We like to say that Zoe had a lot to do and was in a big hurry to get here and do it. A late walker, Zoe made up for lost time once she gained her footing in the world, dancing, tumbling, and climbing on and over everything in sight. The world was her obstacle course, and she scaled furniture and counters, whether it was in our home or elsewhere.

She was also an early talker, speaking full sentences at her one-year pediatric appointment, and seemed to be making up for the silence of monasteries worldwide, chatting up anyone and everyone she encountered from dawn until dusk. Her sentences were like Mad Libs. She once told her daycare teacher, "I want to paint your nose, Miss Liz." To this day, we have no idea what prompted that string of words.

On top of her conversational skills, Zoe's signature twist on life was creating a cast of imaginary family members.

Not content with an imaginary friend (or, evidently, the cast of characters she was born into), she created for her entertainment (and now yours!) an extensive imaginary family.

The firstborn was Joey from Africa. Not Joe. Not Joey. Joey from Africa.

Joey from Africa arrived in our family when Zoe was about two. She and Ruth had been asking me for a little brother. My pregnancies were difficult at best, life-threatening at worst. I knew a third child wasn't in the cards, and I wasn't in the business of giving false hope with vague, placating statements like "Maybe someday" or "We will see what God provides" because "someday"' was outright mythical and I was certain that God was not choosing me as the vessel for The Second Coming.

Instead, I said, "Our family is as big as it needs to be for us. No baby brothers for us."

While we plan (or not), God laughs. In my case, God laughed His Hairy Ass off and sent us Joey from Africa.

Joey from Africa joined the clan one afternoon as we were leaving the house. His arrival was quick and sudden and announced by Zoe's screaming at me when I tried to close the car door.

"MAMA, WAIT!!! WAIT! WAIT WAITWAITWAIT!! Joey from Africa is coming with us to the park! Come on, Joey from Africa, sit next to me."

"Does Joey need a car seat?" I said calmly as if speaking to invisible siblings was an everyday occurrence.

"Joey from AFRICA!" Zoe clarified. The "duh" was implied.

I've said it before, and I'll say it again: Stockholm Syndrome begins at home, and it was my sympathizing with my captor that led me to say nonchalantly, "Okay, does Joey from AFRICA need a car seat?"

"No, he doesn't."

"Good. I don't have one."

Curious about our surprise passenger, I asked, "Who is this Joey from Africa kid anyway?"

"He's our imaginary brother," replied Zoe.

"Of course, he is," I replied. Defeated but determined to soldier on in the face of this latest fuckery, I took a deep breath, closed the car door, and walked around to the driver's seat, where I resumed my role as Juber (Judi + Uber) and took our family (plus one) to the park.

They say insanity is doing the same thing over and over and expecting a different result. Much the way I thought Hanukkah celebrations were a one-and-done deal for our family, I naively presumed Joey from Africa's appearance was a mere cameo.

Boy, was I wrong, for Joey from Africa soon joined the cast of Life with the McLaughlins as a regular.

Joey from Africa sat with us at each meal but brought his own dinnerware; I like to think he was a bit of a fancy guy, seated with fine china and a candelabra. Like Zoe, who we say "was born hungry," Joey from Africa had a voracious appetite and wasn't a picky eater. He cleaned up after himself, which put him in the running for Favorite Family Member since no one else (including Dada) contributed to post-meal tidying up.

Like most kids, Joey from Africa enjoyed his screen time. He watched *Beauty and the Beast* on loop and joined Zoe in exclaiming, "The Beast turned into a people!" with great surprise at the end of the movie each and every time.

At bedtime, he retired to his imaginary bedroom, which I envisioned to be a not-so-humble abode akin to something from *MTV Cribs*. He kept it neat, so I didn't care what it looked like or what was going on in there.

Much to my relief, Joey from Africa was a good road trip buddy. Unlike his sisters, he'd get in the car when asked and kept the girls occupied on our trips to Nana Cat's house. Without him, bedlam ensued, with incessant bickering and the battle cry of "Are we there yet?" so I was grateful to have Joey from Africa tag along. His favorite place to go was the nearby zoo, and Zoe reported that Joey from Africa liked flamingos best.

Often mentioned but never seen, I soon began to talk about Joey from Africa like any other member of the family. He blended right in.

"I'm going to Target. Does Joey from Africa want goldfish crackers?"

"Does Joey from Africa have any laundry? I'm bringing a load downstairs."

By Christmas, I was ready to get him a stocking, only to find out he was gone.

"Joey from Africa went on vacation," Zoe announced at breakfast, apropos of nothing.

"Where did he go? Back to Africa?"

"He didn't say."

"Is he in an undisclosed location with Dick Cheney? Is he coming back?"

"No. He's not coming back. I don't know Dick Cheney."

"I hope he doesn't forget to write."

In my mind, Joey from Africa went back to Africa because he didn't like the cold weather here.

Strangely enough, I missed him.

But the next chapter of our adventures in Imaginary Family Planning commenced with the arrival of Zoe's imaginary cousins: Jack and Lyndia. Not Linda. Not Lydia. Lyndia.

"They are from the land of Orsica," Zoe explained.

Orsica. Not Corsica. Not Baby Orca. Orsica. Where the hell this was nobody knows.

"Is that near where Joey from Africa lives?" I asked.

"No, he's just on vacation!" Zoe replied, annoyed that I wasn't getting the story straight.

"Sounds permanent to me. Anyway, how old are Jack and Lyndia?"

"Today, they are seven and eight."

"Do their ages change each day?"

"Sometimes."

"What are they doing today?"

"Fighting with each other."

"Like arguing?"

"No, like with their fists."

By this time, Zoe was in a preschool/daycare, so I had started to wonder if she had witnessed someone hitting another person at school and her imaginary cousins were her proxy for understanding it.

"I hope no one got hurt!"

"No, they ended it."

Then I began to learn that Jack and Lyndia were, well, not your typical imaginary cousins.

I give you the following scene, also known as "Exhibit A:"

Scene: in the car, driving to God-knows-where.

Zoe: KITTY ON FIRE!!! KITTY ON FIRE!!!! KITTY ON FIRE!!!!

Me, coming to a screeching halt: What is the matter with you?!?!? Where do you see a kitty on fire?!?!!

Zoe: Oh, it's just a game.

Me: THERE IS NO GAME CALLED "KITTY ON FIRE"!!!

Zoe: Yes, there is. Jack and Lyndia taught it to me.

Me [grasping steering wheel, taking a deep breath]: It is not a game for the car.

Zoe: Oh, okay. You hear that, guys? NO KITTY ON FIRE GAME IN THE CAR!

Or, as my friend, Moe points out, in a crowded theater.

Jack and Lyndia learned when to keep a low profile, and much like the infamous gangster, Whitey Bulger, who was on the lam for years, Jack and Lyndia soon mastered the art of hiding in plain sight.

For instance, when we were moving, I didn't hear anything about Jack and Lyndia, except that they were still around, and Zoe would play with them. This was helpful. We were busy, and Jack and Lyndia kept Zoe occupied.

Just when I thought we were safe from Jack and Lyndia's antics, I heard that Jack was back. I didn't know he left, but then again, he is imaginary.

"He has marshmallows. And a gun," Zoe informed me.

"I know I always like my sugary treats with a side of ammunition."

"Well, Mama, you do have that picture of you holding a gun."

This is true. We have several vintage-style photos around the house, and in all of them, I am the character with a gun. I look unusually happy with my firearms, which could make one wonder if I was perhaps premeditating a crime. One more thing for the girls to blame me for in therapy, I guess.

However, in a plot twist no one could have expected, never mind written, Jack returned to Casa McLaughlin solo.

"Where's Lyndia?"

"Lyndia is dead."

"How did she die?"

"Jack set her on fire."

Suddenly, my enthusiasm for the Second Amendment didn't seem so noteworthy. Perhaps we had an imaginary escaped felon on our hands.

"Maybe Lyndia will come back?"

"Yes. Maybe with their grandpa and Jack will be in big trouble."

"Well, let's hope they start carrying fire extinguishers."

And a good defense attorney.

These tales were becoming a mix of a Mexican soap opera and an ABC Afterschool Special.

And a few days later, they were served with a side of Jerry Springer.

"LYNDIA IS HAVING A BABY!!" Zoe announced in the same tone reserved for "SANTA CAME!"

While I didn't expect to become an imaginary grandma so soon in my parenting career, I was delighted to learn that Lyndia had not only risen from the dead but had also managed to conceive.

"That's great. Does she know who the father is?" I say, head in hands, exhausted by the possibilities. To boot, it was only 7 a.m.

"It's her grandpa."

"Okay. NO. Lyndia's grandpa CANNOT be the father of the baby. NO."

"Jack is the daddy?"

"No."

"Then she doesn't know."

I had precisely zero interest in hosting an imaginary paternity test, so instead I asked, "Can't she just get a puppy?"

"Maybe she is getting a puppy."

Much like the song by the band America, "A Horse with No Name," Lyndia's puppy remained anonymous.

Zoe was downright shameless in sharing stories of Jack and Lyndia with others, not caring when or where or with whom she was. Thankfully, one of these disclosures took place with our dear family friend, Mrs. Poole, who is a retired school teacher and principal, and the Pied Piper of Children. The Irony of Ironies was that Zoe chose Sunday School Singalong to tell Mrs. Poole about Jack and Lyndia.

In between songs like "Jesus Loves Me," I watched Zoe regale Mrs. Poole with tales of Jack and Lyndia with the fervor of an evangelical minister admonishing sinners on Sunday.

Mrs. Poole is magical in that she listens in a way that makes you feel like you are the only person on earth who is speaking. Her genuine focus and care leave you feeling so good, like you are the smartest, most amazing person in the world. To bear witness to her devotion to your own child is a marvel to watch.

In my case, given what the Dynamic Duo was capable of, it also invoked sheer terror.

God threw me a freebie that day because it turns out that Mrs. Poole found Zoe's tale hilarious.

As Mrs. Poole told me, "Zoe said she was sooooo tired because Jack and Lyndia and their small band, who play piano and drums very loud, were hosting a singalong until the wee hours of the morning."

I simply gathered from all this that Lyndia had been resurrected *General Hospital*-style and that she gave her baby up for adoption.

But, out of love for Mrs. Poole, I kept those details to myself.

When Zoe was about five, she made an announcement about Jack and Lyndia that no one, least of all I, could have anticipated.

"Mama, I have to tell you something: Jack and Lyndia aren't real."

My jaw dropped, and my eyes bugged out of my head.

"What?" I asked.

"Jack and Lyndia? My imaginary cousins? They are made up."

"What do you mean?" I begin to tear up as if learning the family dog died.

Zoe leaned in toward me and slowly explained, "They are PRETEND, you know, like MADE UP?" She ended her explanation with a grand gesture and arms extended, palms facing up in the "Are you kidding me?" stance.

In a whirlwind of emotion, I pulled myself together and said, "Oh, honey, of course, I know that. I was just kidding with you."

"Yep. They are not real."

"Well, I am going to miss them," and then I started to cry, as in UGLY CRY with snot and tears all mixing up on my face.

At the same time, I was agog. I couldn't believe I was this upset about IMAGINARY, GUN-TOTING, PYROMANIAC CHILDREN WITH BABY DADDIES OF UNKNOWN ORIGIN WHO ROSE FROM THE DEAD!

Distraught beyond all reason and belief, I called "my person," my friend Carrie, the one who, if I showed up with a dead body, would quietly gather a shovel and help me bury it. Except for today, the bodies were imaginary and her shovel unbridled sympathy.

"Zoe just told me that Jack and Lyndia are imaginary, and I am ready to sit shiva," I wept into the phone.

"I will join you," said Carrie, who sat silent as I cried.

When you lose a parent at a young age, it imprints your grief. You find yourself thinking of that parental loss each time you lose a loved one.

Even if the loss is an imaginary person.

But to me, there's more at play with why losing Jack and Lyndia provoked me so intensely.

There's, of course, the loss of Zoe's innocence. Her imagination was so vivid, all-encompassing, and full of life. To me, Zoe's unfettered enthusiasm for creating stories around these characters and her unapologetic zeal for sharing them was downright miraculous. It also was a gift in that it offered me the chance to be a child again.

The insanity of the family I was born into makes for great storytelling fodder, but the price I paid was that I had to grow up fast. As a result, when I became a mom, preserving my children's childhood became a pillar of my parenting.

I joke that "Stockholm Syndrome begins at home," in that we sympathize with our tiny captors, but truth be told, I cherished the chance to dive into the waters of Zoe's imagination and ride the waves alongside her while also protecting her from the inevitable: growing up.

So when she announced Jack and Lyndia's imaginary status, she was declaring her own passage to being a "big girl."

And I, her willing captor, needed to do so too.

I'm not nostalgic for much of early parenting. I'm not one of those moms who says, "I wish they could stay little." I love watching my kids grow. But I will miss Joey from Africa, Jack and Lyndia, and their not-so-small band for the rest of my life.

Their imaginary lives were a blessing.

Shit in the Sandbox

Every mother has a hallmark story of embarrassment that is uniquely hers. My Mother, Mary H., once forgot my brother at the playground next to the neighborhood grocery store, where she popped in one afternoon to get a few items for dinner. While this may seem a common maternal error, Mary H.'s singular shame was that she only realized she'd forgotten him when I asked where he was, three hours after she got home and 10 minutes before dinner was served.

My own Most Embarrassing Mom Moment also involves the playground, and while I didn't lose a kid, I did lose my dignity on one Sunday morning in 2007.

The scene of the crime was Robbins Park in Arlington. Like many suburban playgrounds, Robbins Park is absolutely swarming with children by 7:30 in the morning, seven days a week. I think we were there around 9:30. The girls were four and two at the time.

As was customary for me, I rarely went anywhere without another parent in tow. On this day, Kim Ruane had the dubious honor of being my partner in crime. Her son, Miles, was an integral part of my parenting strategy, as he had the ability to exhaust an army of people with his energy. I know that I thank Jesus Christ Almighty that she was there. I'm not entirely sure that she felt the same way at the end of the day, but let's not get ahead of the story.

The kids were enjoying themselves on the slide and the swings, and Kim and I sat on a bench watching them from afar. Zoe, my two-year-old, was in the midst of potty training. She also was in the midst of serious sensory issues and could at any time decide to take off all her clothes. On this particular day, I was lucky in that she only pulled down her pants, pulled off her diaper, and said, "Me no need this!" then pulled her pants back up and proceeded to continue to play on the playground.

As I tossed her diaper in the trash, I noticed that she was making her way toward the sandbox on the opposite side of the park from where we were sitting. I kept an eye on her, alternating with Ruth, who was (of course) nowhere near the sandbox but rather on the slide.

A little while later, I noticed that Zoe was standing up, wiggling like she had something on her that made her uncomfortable. I immediately thought, "Oh, she wet herself," and proceeded to walk over to her at the sandbox.

"Hey, baby girl, you okay?" I asked as I picked her up. I patted her bum, and she was dry.

"Me go poopie," she replied.

"Oh, you have to go poopie?"

"No, I GO poopie. Right there," and she pointed to the sandbox, where LO AND BEHOLD THERE WAS A GIANT PILE OF POOP.

Yes, Virginia, the wiggly dance I witnessed was Zoe shaking poop down her pant leg. And now it was in a pile. A very neat pile, I might add, IN THE MIDDLE OF THE SANDBOX.

I stood there, frozen in my tracks. I looked to my right, then my left, like you see cops do when they are entering a room where there may be a killer. Except instead of a gun, I was holding a toddler.

The coast was clear. This appeared to be a crime with no witnesses. I contemplated leaving the pile of poop in the hope that someone would blame it on an animal. But by then, because children have no sense of The Art of the Alibi, Zoe announced very loudly, "I WENT POOPIE IN THE SANDBOX, MAMA! IT RIGHT THERE!"

I ran back to Kim, who by now figured something was up.

Probably because I was running with my child in my arms like I was being chased by a bear (who had perhaps pooped in the woods but not today).

Kim: "I am terrified right now."

Me: "Okay, listen, keep a straight face. Poker face. Do not react. Zoe just shit in the sandbox."

Kim: "Oh my god, I cannot believe what you are saying to me right now."

Me: "I know. I have to clean it up. Here, take Zoe. I am going to clean it up and then we are going to leave. No one has to know."

Except in the time it took me to grab a plastic bag and head back to the sandbox, approximately 4,000 people were gathered around it like a town meeting was taking place. The crowd was four people deep. Kids were playing, and no one seemed to notice THE GIANT PILE OF SHIT IN THE SANDBOX.

And because I felt guilt like I never knew before or since, I decided I was going to forge through the crowd and clean up after my child.

"Oh, excuse me, pardon me, don't mind me," I chanted while I made my way to the poop pile. (Did I mention it was approximately 90 degrees? Were these parents COMATOSE?!?! How could you not SEE OR SMELL THIS GIANT PILE OF SHIT?!?!!!)

And as I swooped in to gather the pile of poop, I looked up and saw someone I knew. Not a friend but more of an acquaintance. I waved with one hand while gathering the shit a la "doggie poop bag" style in my other hand, saying, "Oh, don't mind me! Just cleaning up my kid's poop!"

I never saw her again. Probably not by fate, more by design, namely hers.

I calmly left the sandbox, tossed the bag, and returned to Kim, who managed to get all of the kids buckled up in the car and where she uttered these immortal words:

"Judi, you could become the President of the Free World, but today, you are the mom whose kid shit in the sandbox."

Keeping it humble, folks. Keeping it real.

EPILOGUE: I did not return to this park for THREE YEARS. I finally made a pilgrimage with Zoe just before she started kindergarten. I wore a giant sunhat and Jackie O-style glasses, and brought a plastic baggie, just in case, all while bargaining with Jesus and God and all the angels in the sky that no one would recognize me or my child. No one did.

Wifey, My Wifey!

Ask any mother what they wish for in life, and most will respond, "I need a wife." I have been lucky enough to have one. Her name is Raleigh, and she is magical.

Raleigh and I met through her grandmother, Annie, who was my neighbor at the time. I was wearily pushing my five-month-old and two-year-old in the stroller on a scorching hot summer afternoon, praying for the sweet release of death (or at least a nap), when I encountered Annie and Raleigh hanging out on Annie's porch.

"Bring me those babies!" Annie demanded.

You do what Annie tells you and ask questions later.

Raleigh introduced herself and immediately asked to hold Zoe, who snuggled against her without a moment's hesitation. Suddenly, Ruth crawled out of the stroller to sit with Raleigh. My children did not do these things; Zoe cried with everyone, and Ruth wouldn't talk to her own family members.

Clearly, their response to Raleigh was a sign. I knew exactly what I needed to do.

"Raleigh, would you like to babysit my kids? Like, today? For maybe an hour or two? I could use help while I make dinner."

"Sure. I'd love to."

Cathy, Raleigh's mom, joined us just in time to hear my plea of desperation, and the look of shock on her face prompted me to say, "Sorry. I should probably have asked you if that's okay. I don't have much experience hiring babysitters."

As evidenced by my asking a teenager I have known for less than 15 minutes.

Cathy only objected to Raleigh's compensation. "She's never babysat! You don't have to pay her!"

"Well, she can learn with me. I never mothered small people, so we will figure it all out. And of course, I'll pay her."

So Raleigh came home that afternoon and played with my kids. They loved her. I asked her to come again a few days later. And then a few days later after that. She kept showing up. The kids continued to be happy. I continued to make dinner, go to the grocery store, or sometimes just go for a walk. Or take a nap.

Within a year, Raleigh was babysitting while I worked part-time from home and for the occasional date night.

My girls became so attached to Raleigh that as they got older, they would ask me to invite her to visit. Raleigh became so enamored of them that she often would stop by just to hang out with us. My babies became her babies, and we'd rejoice in their milestones together. Raleigh watched them grow from cribs to big girl beds, rejoiced with them when Santa came (bearing menorahs!), and applauded them for earning their black belt in karate.

Raleigh was also front and center for life's challenges too. When Ruth was diagnosed with celiac disease, I called Raleigh to tell her, and before I said a word beyond "hello," she knew I needed her. "Are my babies okay? What can I do?" And without a moment's hesitation, she learned all there was to learn about managing gluten and keeping Ruth safe and healthy. She cultivated a signature dish that the girls begged for: Annie's brand boxed mac and cheese, which we called "Bunny Pasta" in reference to the rabbit-shaped macaroni. Only Raleigh could make Bunny Pasta the way the girls liked it. To this day, I don't know what else she threw in there besides love.

Over time, Raleigh's status rose from "babysitter to "third parent," the only person we'd turn to when Mick and I would spirit away overnight for some quality time together. We always knew the girls were in excellent hands, but I knew the day would come when their familiarity with Raleigh would breed mischief.

That day is known in our family as "Wedding-gate."

Mick and I were heading to an out-of-town wedding in Newport, a trip we were both looking forward to because it meant AN ENTIRE WEEKEND AWAY. I was particularly excited to be dressed in something other than yoga pants and a t-shirt and had gone to such great lengths to look outstanding that I joked I put more work into this wedding than I did my own—a new dress, high-heeled shoes, jewelry, the works. I went so far as to have my hair professionally done the morning of the wedding at a nearby salon that I had booked months in advance.

Coiffed and sleek in a Ralph Lauren dress that, frankly, people are still talking about a decade later, I was ready to enjoy this wedding and time with my husband.

And for the record: Yes, "time with my husband" is a euphemism here, people. You all know what I'm talking about.

So there we were, sipping champagne on the grounds of a Newport mansion on a beautiful summer day, basking in the sunshine in the cool ocean breeze when Mick excused himself to take a phone call.

A few minutes later, as I was in the middle of telling a story about God-knows-what, Mick appeared, ashen-faced and somber, and announced to our group, "I need to go home. Ruth needs me."

Thinking something terrible had happened, I said, "What's wrong? Did she eat gluten by accident? Did she fall down? What did Raleigh say?"

"Oh, Raleigh didn't call. Ruth did."

To this day, I am grateful that I was surrounded by other mothers because our collective Bullshit Detector went into overdrive as we all said, "RUTH called?"

"Yes, Ruth. She needs me," Mick replied as if the president had called.

"She NEEDS you?" I said with suspicion. "Let me call Raleigh and find out what's going on."

Raleigh naturally picked up right away and greeted me with, "I'm so sorry. I know Ruth called Mick."

"That's okay; tell me what's going on."

Breathlessly and in a panic, Raleigh regaled me with Ruth's tale of woe.

"Well, I told the girls that we could go for ice cream after they clean up their toys, but Ruth won't cooperate because she said Zoe made this mess, and when I said we could do it together, she said she was going to call her dad, but I thought she was bluffing, and I guess she wasn't."

"No, she wasn't. By the way, congratulations! Believe it or not, she loves you more than ever because she's pushing the boundaries with you. Kids only do that with people they trust implicitly. You're doing exactly as I would have, and you can stand your ground."

"I'm so sorry; I wanted you and Mick to have a good time."

"Oh, we're having a good time, and that trend will continue. I'll call you this afternoon to see how things panned out, but if it gets to be really weary on you, don't worry about the toys. Some battles aren't worth waging."

And then I calmly clicked my phone shut and turned to Mick and the group of women. I was smart enough to stick around and told him, "She's fine. She's not getting her way, and she thinks you're going to change that."

"I think I should go home. Jackie is leaving here in about an hour, and I can catch a lift with him."

Furious inside, I also found Mick's devotion endearing; he hated that Ruth was sad (or was insomuch as she portrayed herself to be). But I also knew if he went home, he'd set a terrible precedent in undermining Raleigh.

Fury won out as I said, "If you go home with Jackie, you will be living with Jackie."

The Other Mothers Greek Chorus chimed in:

"You can't let a nine-year-old steamroll you like that!"

"Are you seriously going to leave Judi here by herself? You guys never get away together!"

Soon some dads chimed in with much more colorful language that I'll spare you from but involved comparing Mick to a kitty cat and pointing out that I looked really hot and what the hell was wrong with him.

Realizing he'd get more grief for leaving than staying, Mick remained.

Up to this point, I realized that the relationship Raleigh and I had forged defied definition, but Wedding-gate made it clear that the one and only name that made sense was "Wifey."

Wifey is a shared term, and Raleigh and I still refer to each other that way. And while the girls are long past needing a sitter, Raleigh and I remain in each other's lives, filling empty spaces in one another's hearts. We are confidantes, and I've been blessed to witness her milestones: I watched her graduate high school and then venture on to college and, most recently, graduate school. I've met her significant others and hold the esteemed role as the person she tells about a relationship before it's "Facebook official," when she celebrates career developments or the latest "I'm moving" update.

And, of course, like all spouses, we share inside jokes. Our favorite: I am not only her Wifey but her "pimp," referring to or serving as reference for nannying gigs. But unlike an actual pimp, I don't muscle up to her clients with violent threats and demand that they pay up a la Paulie Walnuts on *The Sopranos*. Although if she asked me to, I absolutely would!

A few years ago, Raleigh and I started a tradition of having at least one "date night" for us, "The Wifeys." We talk about anything and everything but the kids. After all, we need a break from them too.

I'm not really sure how this happened, but Raleigh is now 31 years old. Not long ago, my sleep-deprived, haggard neighbor stopped me on my afternoon walk to ask if one of my kids could babysit her brood. She had the desperate glazed-donut eyes that I remember having myself. Much like Raleigh's mom all those years ago, I barked out "Of course!" and then watched, tearful, as my kiddo trotted off to become this tired mom's Wifey. Ah, the circle of life. And I know that kid will be an excellent Wifey. After all, she learned from the best.

The circle of life continues, Dear Wifey. You are one in a million, and I'm so glad you're mine.

Animal Husbandry and
Other Adventures

As I sit here on a rainy Sunday morning, Mick regales me with the farming portion of The Tullaugh Update, his weekly call home to Donegal. I already know what the weather is, who's dead, and who's sick—no human births to report. However, the cattle update focused on calving.

Eddie, Mick's older brother and patriarch of the McLaughlin Clan, has cows that are with calf (pregnant) and some that are not. Given the subsidies he gets, he has to have all cows with calf or bring them to the factory for slaughter. Cattle produce one way or another.

Mick described to me how farmers determine if a cow "took the AI" (they bring an ultrasound machine to see who's knocked up).

The AI is the artificial inseminator. He drives around with a vat of bullshot (not "shit," "shot," as in "bull semen") on dry ice, and he impregnates the cows with a vial insert. I know this how? Because I've watched him.

Witnessing the AI remains my claim to fame in Mick's family. I am the only woman who has watched the AI "do his business." Trust me, it's not glamorous, but as a city gal, I had to see it to believe it. Mostly because when Mick told me this was the method, I thought he was pulling my leg. He assured me he was not and promised that if the opportunity arose (pun intended), I would have a front-row seat to the whole production.

So on my first visit to the family farm in 1997, I made it my mission to see what in the Sam-Hill was happening here so I could report back to my fellow Americans. I embedded myself in farm life to learn all there was to learn about the life of the AI, the way Hunter S. Thompson, founder of the gonzo journalism movement, rode alongside the Hell's Angels to learn all there was to learn about motorcycle gangs.

As the first American to infiltrate Mick's family, I was already considered a minor celebrity, but once I announced my fascination with the AI, I was viewed as more of an eccentric, like Howard Hughes.

"You want to see the AI?" Mick's father, Big John, asked incredulously.

"Yes! This is fascinating to me! I have so many questions! I always thought cows just, you know, DID IT. I had no idea there was a proxy!"

Big John looked at Mick with an expression that seemed to say, "Of all the Americans, you had to find this one?" Mick simply shrugged.

"Women don't usually want to see this," Big John explained.

"I'm not your typical woman," I said.

"I can see that, Jo-Jo." Mick's father had taken to calling me Jo-Jo for reasons that remain a mystery to me as much as my fascination with the AI was to him. And I called him "Big John," which, incidentally, is how everyone addressed him. Nicknames are common in Clonmany, a story we can get into another time, but I can tell you John's made sense because he was six feet tall and built like a brick house.

Sadie, Mick's mom, sat in her rocker by the fire, quietly shaking her head, giggling. "I can't believe you came all the way from America, and this is what you want to see," she said.

"Welcome to me!" I responded with glee, arms spread out in the "ta-da" pose.

As I ventured into my new obsession, the first piece of shocking news (to me) was that all of the AI festivities are kicked off with a phone call. Well, really, they're kicked off by a cow mooing, but since cows can't dial a phone, the farmer calls on the cow's behalf.

On the morning we heard the cow mooing, I, the newly-appointed Town Crier of Artificial Insemination, ran into the kitchen and asked Big John, "Are you gonna call the AI now?"

No one was more excited to hear a cow moo than me.

Amused by my childlike enthusiasm for what was, to him, a routine matter, Big John joined me in my excitement by jumping up and heading to the phone.

"You ready for this, Jo-Jo?"

"I have been waiting my whole life for this!" I said like we were about to call Santa Claus.

I stood alongside Big John and waited with bated breath to hear what mystifying conversation was about to take place.

The next revelation in this fertility journey was that there are three questions one must answer when you call AI:

When the cow started mooing, which in our case was less than 10 minutes before Big John called, he simply said, "This morning."

What breed of cow, which in our case was a Holstein.

And my favorite:

First time or repeat? Yes, Virginia, the AI guarantees his product! If it didn't work the first time, you get a freebie.

Big John answered all these questions with his signature deadpan delivery while also looking at me for signs of what I was about to say next.

He didn't have to wait long.

"What's going to happen now? What did the AI say?" I asked, excited to hear what secrets were revealed on the other end of the phone.

"He said we're gonna wait. Lots of cows mooing today, Jo-Jo. The AI will be here when he gets here."

"When's that going to be?"

"When he arrives," Big John said, leaving me to stand by the phone table while he returned to his (now cold) cup of tea.

Undeterred, I staged a one-woman sit-in by the kitchen window, intent on meeting Joe Greene, the AI on call, and witnessing how baby cows are made.

I sat there, gazing down the road, like a puppy awaiting its human, perking up in my seat each time a car drove by.

I must have looked to Sadie like a forlorn child awaiting a playmate. She implored me, "Jo-Jo, you aren't really missing anything by watching Joe Greene. Maybe you and Micky should go out for the afternoon. It's a beautiful sunny day. It's going to rain later. You'll wish you'd gone out."

Downtrodden and disappointed, I relented, and Mick and I hopped in the car to do some sightseeing of a non-farming kind.

As we hit the fork in the road, a small hatchback vehicle sped past us, which Mick identified as the (in)famous Joe Greene.

"Turn this car around right now! I am not missing this!" I shouted.

We sped back up the road and screeched into the driveway *Dukes of Hazard*-style. As I hopped out before we came to a full stop, I could see Sadie in the doorway, yelling, "Hurry! Joe Greene is very quick!"

Aren't they all?

Breathless from running across the field, I met up with Big John, who introduced me to Joe. "This is my son's girlfriend. She's here all the way from Boston to see this."

Joe, without missing a beat, replied in a deadpan voice, "There must be nothing to do in Boston."

"Not like this there isn't. Let's get this show on the road!" I replied with glee.

Joe, by this time, had a vial of bullshot ready. He put it between his teeth (!!!!), jumped into the pen with the cow, put one hand inside her, yanked the vial from his mouth, and shoved it in.

The cow bellowed. I was speechless. My father-in-law shook his head and paid Joe. Mick, who had strolled in after it was all over, stood there, threw his head back, and laughed as I remained agog at what I had just witnessed.

For the remainder of the trip, Sadie introduced me to everyone as "Micky's American girlfriend" and quickly added, "Did you hear she watched the AI?" Then I, in my newly-appointed role as Weirdest New Family Member, would regale everyone with the tale of what so few had witnessed.

Sadie always managed to add, "I've been on that farm over 40 years and never once watched the AI. Not once! Judi was here three days, and there she is, watching something we women wanted nothing to do with!"

I like to make an impression like Sharpie marker on a white couch.

Since that hallowed day in 1997, I've been making the pilgrimage to the family farm, where I continue to be heralded as a modern-day fertility goddess. On one memorable journey, I got to witness a cow calving, and by that, I mean "We were walking along the road minding our own business when we saw hooves sticking out of a cow in a nearby field."

Content to maintain my role as a bystander, I watched Mick hop a fence, run up to the cow, and pull a calf out.

"Just another day at the office," we'd say.

I've also been woken in the middle of the night to the news that a neighbor's cow is in distress and to watch Mick pull on his clothes to head down the road assist. That time the cow needed a cesarean section, which was performed by the local veterinarian.

But perhaps the story I remember most is the one we talk about least: how Big John met his maker one morning in January when he was killed by a bull.

Yes. A bull.

To me, this story is not only the cruelest of ironies, but it demonstrates Big John's extraordinary strength and fortitude.

Given that the cattle on the family farm are for slaughter, the sign that a cow's or bull's time is up is when the trailer pulls into the field and farmers load the cattle aboard. Big John, accompanied by a few neighbors, was pushing a bull from behind onto the trailer when the bull kicked back and his hoof caught on Big John's belt buckle.

And kicked and kicked and kicked some more.

The other men jumped in to assist, and legend has it that Big John managed to pry the hoof out of his buckle, give the bull one last shove, locked the gate, and said, "Okay, I'm done."

He then proceeded to walk a quarter mile back to the house, change his clothes, and sit down for breakfast.

After his routine tea and scone bread, he casually mentioned to Sadie and Eddie that his stomach hurt and that he should go to the doctor "for a tablet or something."

Eddie drove him to the doctor in the center of town, and as Big John lumbered toward the door, he collapsed. He was rushed to the nearest hospital, which in their region of Donegal was 40 minutes away.

In triage, it was determined that most of Big John's internal organs were shattered beyond recognition. Doctors were able to stabilize him in preparation for a transfer to Dublin, but Big John's big heart gave out and he died six hours later.

Whereas in 2022, you learn of death within seconds, in 1999, it took slightly longer for us to learn of Big John's untimely demise. We were 3,000 miles away in Boston, having just left for work at our respective jobs: me at an office in the financial district and Mick in his backhoe at a construction site.

I had barely got my coat off when Mick called to tell me that one of his sisters called to report that Big John was en route to the hospital. He only told me and kept the news from all of his coworkers, choosing to cope by focusing on the task at hand: digging a hole to replace a sewer line.

What he didn't know was that his boss, Chuck, knew what was

happening, having received a similar phone call from his own sister, who lived down the road from Big John and Sadie. Not much later, Chuck arrived on the job site and approached Mick, who knew what Chuck had to say but didn't want to hear it.

Chuck also didn't want to say it, but as someone who grew up alongside Big John and Sadie, Chuck was family, so truly there was no better person to break the news.

"I don't know how to tell you this…" Chuck began.

"He died, didn't he?" said Mick.

The Irish are not known for open displays of emotion, and Mick epitomizes the archetype. Yet, minutes later, when I answered my phone again, all I could hear were heart-wrenching, primal sobs. No words. Only tears of a man who was robbed of his father, who didn't get a chance to say goodbye.

I stood up from my desk in the middle of a trading room-style office and, clutching my phone to my ear, openly wept.

We were 3,000 miles away from Donegal, but we might as well have been on the moon.

I trust that Big John is in Heaven doing what he loved most: tending to cattle, bringing them into the world twice: overseeing the art of the AI and then assisting in birthing them—or sipping the finest Irish whiskey and regaling anyone who'd listen with tales of his youth. Or all of the above. He will always be missed and never forgotten. I couldn't erase that AI scene from my mind even if I tried.

I always think of these stories when Mick is talking with Eddie, and now that Mick and I are no longer a couple, I have to say, I miss these updates.

The Nephew Who
Loved Me First

In 1997, I met a little boy, my boyfriend's nephew, at a family wedding in Ireland. We took a picture. Legend has it he spent the next 10 months talking to that picture every night, recalling his day "to Doody."

We met again after I married his uncle. He asked me if I would come to his wedding someday. I told him, of course I would. He made me promise I would wear a big hat.

We met again when his grandad died. The little boy was heartbroken, cried about how unfair it was. And it was unfair because Grandad got taken suddenly, without warning. The boy asked me where grandad went, and I told him he was in Heaven, but we could come to where we stood, at his gravesite, any time we wanted to talk to him. He replied, "Heaven already? That was wild fast!"

The little boy was sometimes mistaken for my son. I always corrected those who thought so but was secretly proud of the error.

We met year after year, and he'd always come straight to me when we walked in the door. He sat on my lap and asked me questions about what I did in America for a job and if I drove a car.

One time he noticed my hair was different.

"Yes, it's longer than last time."

"It's a different color too!"

His granny, my mother-in-law, said she wished she had a camera for these exchanges; they were so honest and funny.

When I was expecting my first child, I asked the boy if he thought it was a girl or boy.

"I think it's twins!" he said mischievously and ran away laughing.

The boy loved his little American cousin and her sister when she came a few years later and babysat for me when I asked, even after one very late night out.

The boy and I have our inside jokes and can tell a whole story with just one look, like the epic tale of "passing the Top Shop for the fiftieth time tonight!" which sends us both into uproarious laughter, recalling our multiple trips up and down the same road, passing the same Top Shop gas station, in an attempt to get out of the house so Granny could rock infant Ruth to sleep in peace.

Now the boy is a man. He's found a partner he loves, whom I've yet to meet and whom I've taken to calling Marty Glass, a reference to Jan Brady's imaginary boyfriend, George Glass, on *The Brady Bunch*. We can still make each other laugh until milk comes out of my nose.

I get teased that he is my favorite. But he is simply the Nephew Who Loved Me First. And I am his FYA: Favorite Yankee Auntie.

His uncle and I have made the difficult decision to divorce, and it shattered my heart and soul to tell him. We mostly message via WhatsApp, and I remember the river of tears I shed when I broke the news.

"You will always be my FYA and I will always be the Nephew Who Loved You First," he told me.

And so it is written.

The Dead Are the Priority

When you are married to an Irish immigrant, trips to the home-land are part of the package, as is culture shock. As a woman of Irish heritage, I knew enough of some traditions, like the importance of knowing how to brew a cup of tea and empty your cup-boards to feed guests, no matter how many times they tell you they're not hungry.

However, the one tradition I cannot fathom, no matter how many trips I've made to the Motherland, is the peculiar tradition of obituaries on the radio.

I will give you a moment to reflect on that idea.

As with most traditions, there is a history behind them. First, the region where Mick is from, Donegal, is a rural, close-knit com-munity of farmers and tradesmen who are late adopters of technol-ogy. As such, the mailman was typically the person who gave you news of who died. But as time passed, trucks replaced bicycles as the mode of transport for the mailman, and with it, the expectation that he would cover more territory, so less time to chat. Hence, obits on the radio (were born?).

My mother-in-law, Sadie, as you can probably imagine, listens to the obits with religious fervor, second only to Mass. No matter what we are all doing, once the clock strikes 10 a.m, we have to shut up, stop everything, and get the hell out of her way as she makes a beeline for the radio to "find out who's dead."

The obits are read with a somber tone, as to be expected, as well as the location of the home where the body will be waked (yes, they still wake at home in Donegal), and the time and location of the burial Mass. The only sounds that are permitted are "tsk tsk tsk" and "Lord have mercy!" but there are times when we are "shocked! shocked, I tell you!" that someone has died. I have been poked in the ribs more than once for talking during this most holy of times.

The first few times I witnessed the obits on the radio, I sat there like a deer in the headlights. Now, as (yet another) testament that Stockholm Syndrome begins at home, I partake in my self-appointed capacity as the person to answer the phone after the obits.

Anytime we visited my in-laws in Ireland, I nominated myself the family receptionist. Because, you see, immediately after the obits are read aloud on the airwaves, Sadie's phone lights up like a Dead People Hotline.

About 30 seconds after the last obit is read, the phone begins to ring with news of who is dead, in case you missed the obits, which of course, has never happened, but you can never be too careful.

But there is more to the post-obit phone calls, and this is where it gets really weird.

You see, where Mick is from, everyone has a nickname. For instance, we are "The Colliers" even though our last name is "McLaughlin." Evidently, because there are so many people with the same last name, they started handing out nicknames to people.

There are also nicknames for first names. In this case, sometimes the names make sense. Sadie's neighbor was "Wee Arthur" because he was small and his name was Arthur. My father-in-law was "Big John" because—you guessed it!—he was named John and he was a big guy. Sometimes they make no sense at all (as you will see shortly) unless you know the story behind the nickname.

The problem with nicknames is that you could go your whole life calling your neighbor one name and never know his or her real name, and then when the obit is read, you don't know its {nickname}, and there is nothing more embarrassing than finding out that you didn't pay respect to the dead, all because you didn't know the person's real name.

A few years ago, a man in the community, whose nickname was "Spoons," died unexpectedly. This was how the obits time went:

{Radio announcer reads "Spoons'" obit, except they use his real name, which to this day, I do not know.}

Sadie: "OH MY GOD! SPOONS IS DEAD!!!"

Me: "Who is Spoons?"

Sadie, looking at me like I just asked who Jesus is: "He played the spoons. That's why we called him 'Spoons!'"

Me: "Was he playing them in the womb? Is that his real name?"

Mick: "Of course not; it's his nickname!"

Me: "What's his real name?"

Sadie: "SHUSH! THE OBITS ARE ON!!!!"

Me: "Sorry."

Then the phone rings.

Me: "Hello?"

Person: "Who's this?"

Me: "Token American relative. How are you?"

Person: "Oh, right, right, right. Good to hear you. When you leaving?"

Me: "Not soon enough."

Person: "SPOONS IS DEAD!"

Me: "Yep. We heard. I'll pass it on."

Next call:

Me: "Hello!"

Person: "SPOONS IS DEAD!!!"

Me: "Still?"

Person: "What?"

Me: "Nothing. We heard. I'll pass it on."

The third call was from my sister-in-law, Bernie, who calls my mother-in-law every single day after the obits.

Me: "Hello! You're next on *Guess Who's Dead?*"

Bernie, unaffected by my greeting: "Oh, hello, Judi! It's Bernie! How's it going?"

Me: "Good. Let me guess. You're calling to tell us Spoons is dead?"

Bernie: "SPOONS IS DEAD?!?!"

Me: "Yep. Let me put Sadie on the phone."

This leads us to the next phase of The Daily Obits: planning our day! Because now we have to go to one or more of these wakes, or "corpse houses" as the family calls them.

Sadie: "You want to come to the corpse house?"

Me: "No, I'm trying to quit."

Sadie: "You'll probably see a lot of people there!"

Me: "I know one who won't notice!"

We recently had a laugh about my social awkwardness around the subject of the daily obits through Facebook, and my nephew Kevin, summed it up perfectly, "Judi, the dead are the priority!"

No truer words were spoken.

A Little Happy, a Little Sad

Today is a happy day and a sad day. I took the girls and two friends to the Stone Zoo. They broke off into pairs, maps in hand, and said they'd meet me at the entrance.

"Oh, okay. Enjoy your time," I said. I was proud of their confidence but a little sad that I wasn't a part of their adventure like I used to be.

We came home and had lunch, and they all hung out upstairs, listening to Taylor Swift. I somehow found time to nap. I was happy about that but a little sad because I used to love to nap with my kids.

I had offered to take the girls to the corner store and get ice cream treats, but they decided to go on their own. I was happy that they could do this; I taught them how to be careful on the windy rats-maze of roads in our neighborhood, to watch out for cars, dogs to avoid, houses that are safe to stop in if something goes awry.

I was also happy to see their friends, whom they've known since infancy and toddlerhood, were going with them because I know that these particular friends will be theirs for life.

But as they walked over the hill, I was a little sad that I wasn't leading the pack anymore and that I wasn't privy to their conversations in all their glorious detail.

So now I'm awaiting their return, hoping they tell me something about their walk, so I can be happy to hear a piece of their day instead of sad that I missed it in order for them to have these tastes of freedom.

Do Not Little

I watched the two toddlers, a boy and girl, probably three and four years old, pushing their tricycles down the street. The boy was calling for his sister to wait for him. Their dad was walking behind, and he saw me admire them.

"Please tell me they will always be this age," he told me.

"Yours will. I heard they installed an upgrade," I replied with a smile. He chuckled.

I am guessing that memory will count as one of that dad's favorites. We all have them. My favorite memories of my daughters are when I picked them up at daycare in the summertime, and they would be playing in the adjacent playground. I'd observe from afar, watching them sharing with friends, laughing and running, and playing games. Their teachers learned to let me announce myself rather than call them to me when I arrived. To observe them in such an uninhibited way always left me in awe and gave me joy. I also knew that time was fleeting, and these moments were my way to hold it still for a little while.

The truth is, I wouldn't want my kids back at that age ever again. I loved my time with them, and I made my best effort to enjoy our days of toddlerhood and the preschool years and to be present for their milestones. I mean, really present; I didn't photograph that much then, instead relying on the kindness of daycare providers and friends who were better skilled at photos before the advent of the iPhone camera.

As my girls got older, I attended their dance recitals and camp variety shows and simply watched. I didn't videotape; instead, I reveled in the moment of watching them express themselves, enjoy their time with their friends, make memories for themselves.

Later, dance lessons were replaced by music lessons—piano for one, voice for the other. I loved going to recitals, listening to the fruits of their labors and the joy they each felt in their accomplishments.

Watching my daughters progress in martial arts has been the most rewarding experience of parenting them thus far. For four and a half years, I witnessed their struggles, their dedication, their unbridled happiness at each belt ceremony. When they achieved black belt, I wept tears of joy for them. I couldn't have been prouder of them.

Except someday, I will be prouder, I will be happier. I will be more excited than I ever was before; because every time I watch them succeed, I think, "I cannot wait to see the next great thing they do."

I know in my "hut" (heart + gut) that this wisdom comes from loss and grief. Bill H. died when I was 17. He didn't see me graduate high school, much less college. He didn't walk me down the aisle, and he never got to witness his grandchildren (although their mischief indicates he's alive and well in another form).

So, instead, I honor him. I've stopped wishing that my kids will stay small, forever preserved in time on their tricycles. I don't want that. To me, celebrating each new milestone beats lamenting the days gone by.

Do not stay little. Grow and let me witness as many phases of your life as humanly possible.

But for the Grace of Goddess
Go I

In 2007, a woman took her preschool-aged children to the local pond. It was a scorcher of a day, and the children were already over-tired and cranky. So was the mom. But she figured that a few hours playing by the water would be enough reprieve for all of them.

The woman saw a friend at the pond. They sat together and watched their children play in the water, no less than 10 feet away. All the children were wearing swim vests. The mom chatted with her friend, catching up on changes in their lives—preschool, work, activities their children were involved in—while watching her children enjoy the water.

The mom turned to say something to her friend, one sentence, maybe two or three. She turned back toward the water. Her younger daughter was face down in the pond, struggling to get her head up. The swim vest caused suction, making it impossible for the toddler to get her head up.

The mom leaped from her seat on her towel, ran as fast as she could, and slid into the water to scoop up her daughter. Her little one looked her mother in the face and simply said, "That was scary."

Her friend comforted her when she returned to where she was sitting, daughter in her arms. People asked if she and her daughter were okay. The mom simply said they were and thanked people for their concern.

That mom was me.

No one reported me to the authorities. No one judged me for taking my eyes away for the split second it took for the unthinkable to transpire.

For years afterward, when I expressed my fear of going near water with my kids, my friends supported me. They did not question when I wouldn't go to the pond. They didn't try to persuade me otherwise. They stood up for me in my resolve to stay away from the place that brought back such terrifying thoughts of "what if?"

My friends could have scolded me or snickered and gossiped about the pond debacle behind my back. They didn't. They provided grace when I needed it most.

It's heartbreaking that—for so many moms—this isn't the case.

We've all witnessed the horrendous mom-shaming that happens on the internet or, worse, in real life. No matter what a mom chooses to do, someone will cast judgment.

"She's a terrible mom for glancing away while the kids swim. How neglectful." Or the opposite: "She's a terrible mom for hovering obsessively and monitoring their every movement. She needs to chill out."

Damned if you do, damned if you don't. Moms can't win. Some people can be unbelievably cruel, and ironically, while we recognize the scrutiny of "society," we rarely acknowledge that the cruelty happens on the playground, in the schoolyard, at the kitchen table, where the moms gather.

But (like my friends), we all have the capacity to be caring and kind and to offer grace.

It took a bit longer for me to learn how to extend that same kindness to myself.

After that hot summer day in 2007, I avoided the pond like it was my job. Not difficult, given we had a pool, which rendered a trip to the pond unnecessary. Why go to the pond when you could cool off right outside your door? My kids also didn't care for the pond water, having gotten sick there on a different occasion (yes, our luck at Wright's is not great).

Then in the summer of 2018, I started going to yoga at the

pond at 8 a.m. on Saturday mornings. Classes were early enough for a peaceful practice and meditation and were held before the pond opened for day visitors.

At first, I was reluctant to attend but decided I would go to one class. If I didn't like being there, I could leave at any time.

I stayed for the entire class. And I continued to attend, week after week.

Gradually, I found myself enjoying the pond in a different way. The mist dissipating from the water, the sun warming my face, and the cool, soft sand between my toes offered an energizing experience. My walks to and from the pond gave me time to reflect on my reframed ritual, and soon, Saturday yoga at Wright's Pond morphed into my favorite moment of each summer weekend.

The next year, I bought a walk-in pass for the season. I bargained with my heart and mind and once again brokered the deal that I would venture there on my terms and give myself permission to leave whenever I wanted.

On my first visit, I sat beneath a tree and read for about an hour but felt a little panicked, so I left.

On the second visit, I sat closer to the shore, thanks to a lovely friend who quietly and lovingly served as my emotional sherpa. We sat with a group of friends for laughs and libations and took a group photo to commemorate our time together.

On the third trip, Mick and I spent a quiet afternoon at Wright's. I read; he napped.

While he snoozed, I strolled to the shore and stepped into the water for the first time in 12 years. I walked the length of the beach, feeling the water on my ankles, then stood still and soaked in the surroundings: children laughing and splashing each other, tiny minnows tickling my feet, sunlight dancing on the water, the scent of sunscreen. And I found myself deeply grateful.

I changed the story. I forgave myself. Peace with the pond was complete. Amen.

The Last Kissy

There's been a quote floating around social media lately that has haunted me to my very core:

"At some point in your childhood, you and your friends went outside to play together for the last time, and nobody knew it."

I wasn't necessarily taken aback by the fact that I missed the last time I hung out with my childhood friends. Rather, it made me think about the "last times" with my kids, like the last time I took them to the zoo.

It was the end of summer vacation, and I corralled a group of kids (including my own two) and headed off for an afternoon of fun. But their definition of "fun" defied my own.

Rather than my leading the pack, they chose to break off into pairs, maps in hand and said they'd meet me at the entrance.

Then later in the day, when I offered to take them all to the corner store for ice cream treats, they again opted to go on their own. I was happy that they could do this; I taught them how to be careful on the windy rats-maze of roads in our neighborhood, to watch out for cars, dogs to avoid, houses that are safe to stop in if something went awry.

But as they walked over the hill, I was a little sad that I wasn't leading the pack anymore and that I wasn't privy to their conversations in all their glorious detail.

I sat on the back deck, awaiting their return, hoping they tell me something about their first walk to the store on their own. Instead of being sad that I missed out on the journey, I chose to celebrate their small taste of freedom.

So much of parenting is caught up in "firsts:" first steps, first words, the first day of school, first dates, etc. that we miss the "last" times: last time you change a diaper, last time they ask you to read a story to them at bedtime, last time you bring them to school.

Coincidentally, or maybe because I have been thinking about these last times, I became aware that Zoe was ending a ritual I have cherished for a long time: Kissy at Drop Off.

"Kissy" is exactly what it sounds like: a kiss goodbye. Zoe had always been an affectionate child and loved to give me a kissy at the bus stop or at drop off at karate or a friend's house or anywhere, really. But now, in seventh grade, as I dropped her at school most mornings on my way to the office, I've watched this ritual creep to a halt.

The first day she didn't give me a kissy was a few days before winter break. I thought it was because she was running late and wanted to get into the building.

The next day I had to ask for a kissy.

That's when I realized; this was the Last Kissy.

Now I wish I never noticed. It would hurt less.

That quote doesn't haunt me anymore; I understand that not knowing the last time is the mind's way of protecting the heart.

Mother of the Year

In yet another spectacular example of mothering mishaps, sit down and get cozy as I regale you with tales related to my alleged tendency to forget my kids in different places.

It is alleged because the whole legend begins with an accusation that was completely unfounded.

Ruth was in kindergarten, and her afternoon sitter, CJ, would take her to her house after school a few days a week, and they would have a snack and do homework while I wrapped up work and picked up Zoe at daycare. One afternoon, our friend, Patrick, came by to talk to CJ's parents and asked Ruth what she was doing at CJ's house.

Ruth looked him straight in the face and said, "Oh, my mom forgot me at the bus stop again."

What the actual fuck? AGAIN? How about I had NEVER DONE THAT?!!?!

Too late, the myth had been established, and I spent the better part of Ruth's early elementary years dispelling the notion that I forgot my kid at the bus stop on a regular basis.

Fast forward to Zoe's kindergarten year. I pull up to the bus stop at my usual time and see the bus and my two kids getting BACK ON IT. I ran faster than OJ Simpson through an airport and got to the bus just in time to get them, and when I did so, the bus driver said, "Oh, I was early today!"

To which both my kids responded, "It's okay. Mama forgets us all the time."

"I HAVE NEVER FORGOTTEN YOU AT THE BUS!!!"

At dinner, the lies continue:

Mick: "How was everyone's day?"

Kids: "Mama forgot us today. The bus driver almost had to bring us back to school."

Me: "That is NOT TRUE! I was running down the street, and I almost LOST MY SHOE running so fast."

Mick: "Nice, Judi."

Me: "SERIOUSLY! I didn't forget them!"

Then it got worse. Not because I started forgetting them. Because OTHER PEOPLE did.

Unfortunately, this seemed to happen disproportionately to Ruth.

Once, a mom forgot to pick up Ruth from a different after-school group but got Zoe.

A different mom was supposed to pick up Ruth at school, and it didn't happen.

Then there was the time that school put Ruth on the bus when they weren't supposed to. Another time, the school didn't put her on the bus when they should have.

Another variation on the theme was a mom picked up my kids at the bus, but my kids didn't know (it was a last-minute schedule change), and they didn't get off the bus, and the mom had to chase the bus to get the kids.

Summer camp created a whole new level of chaos, none of it initiated by me. I had a work meeting that conflicted with camp pickup and asked a dear friend who lived near the camp to get Ruth.

The friend forgot.

I think I subconsciously decided that I could no longer permit this disparate treatment. That was when I started to forget Zoe.

I mean, I am going to get blamed for it anyway, so why not join in?

The first incident was the third-grade field trip to Plimoth Plantation. You'd think I would've remembered having already had one kid partake in this field trip, but motherhood is funny like that: You forget the darndest things!

I was out for a run and stopped in Starbucks afterward when my phone rang. I saw the school phone number and thought, "Oh, maybe the bus is late."

No, dummy, YOU ARE LATE.

The phone call was from (thank Jesus in the sky!) a teacher with whom I was friends and who had a daughter in the same grade. She informed me that Zoe was waiting for me. And I informed her I was nowhere near my car, never mind school. She took mercy on my soul and brought Zoe home for me.

And from there on in, the legend of Judi Forgetting Her Kids Everywhere gained credibility.

And more evidence.

One night, I was sitting around, enjoying a book, listening to some music, when I had a nagging feeling that I had forgotten something. I brushed it off and got ready for bed. I was snug in my bed when I realized, "Oh my god, Zoe is across the street at Maria's house!"

This led to me setting my Facebook statuses to "Someone please remind me to get my kids before bedtime."

When I go in, I go ALL IN.

Luckily for me, my kids have the Mama Tribe, meaning that pretty much everywhere they go, there is one kid whose mother will deposit them back to me. Some call it kismet. I call it good long-range planning. So in the event that I do forget a kid somewhere, there is a very good chance that my child will simply attach herself to another mother and that mom will bring my kid home.

Like sleepaway camp, for instance.

NO, I DID NOT FORGET MY KID AT SLEEPAWAY CAMP!

I almost forgot my kid at sleepaway camp.

Actually, it wasn't really forgetting; it was my thinking she didn't need to be picked up.

Let me explain.

The scene of this (near) crime is, of all places on the planet, Jesus Camp. I signed Zoe up for two weeks, back-to-back. I thought this meant "two consecutive weeks, without interruption." You know, like most camps?

In the weeks leading up to camp, Zoe kept asking me, "Am I coming home in between the two weeks?"

Thinking this was a question from a kid who had never experienced sleepaway camp, I said, "Oh no, honey, you stay the whole two weeks."

Then she asked again a few days later but in a different way.

"Mama, so-and-so's mom is getting a hotel near camp to get so-and-so on Saturday."

"Well, if so-and-so's mom can't live without her kid, that's her problem."

Third time was not a charm.

"Mama, can I come home in between the two weeks at camp?"

Exasperated by the same question, I replied, "If you can catch a lift home, you can come home."

Fast forward to the first Friday of camp. I just happen to be talking with another camp mom, reveling in the fact that I have a Saturday all to myself.

"Well, you know we have to get the kids, right?"

"Will you people stop with this shit about getting kids at camp?"

"No, we have to get them."

"Stop punking me. I know I am reputed to be leaving my kids all over town, but I am not falling for this one."

"Judi. I am serious. They have to get picked up tomorrow."

"Really? I don't think so. I'm going to call camp."

Camp informs me that I am evidently The Only Mother Who Wasn't Planning to Get Her Kid.

I inform the camp that I am The Only Mother Who Is a Paralegal and Can Show Them There Is Nothing About This on Their Website.

I think about Zoe, and I start to feel really guilty. But I assuage my guilt by rationalizing that she will be surprised to see me.

When I arrive at camp the next morning, Zoe looks at me like I have risen from the dead (see what I did there?).

"Hi, honey! I missed you!"

"Hi, Mama, I missed you too."

"You didn't think I was coming, did you?"

"No, Mama. But I had a Plan B. I was going to go home with Zoe P.'s mom. I already arranged it."

Now, if that is not a silver lining, I do not know what is. To know that your little girl can think on her own, not panic, and calmly make a backup plan? THAT, my friends, is priceless, especially considering how people are expected to parent in 2022. Kids have everything short of a microchip in their heads: cellphones with GPS tracking, Uber apps to call a ride if needed.

But where's the fun in that?

Thanks to all the devices, kids today never get "left" or "forgotten" anywhere—and thus, they never have the opportunity to develop crucial life skills like Zoe did! She learned how to advocate for herself and find her own backup ride just in case.

Maybe it's good for kids to be abandoned at a bus stop once in a while. Builds character. Okay, not literally abandoned. But you know what I mean.

Part-Time Lesbian

Over the years, I've hosted what I like to call Oprah's Couch in my living room. Much like when Oprah was on TV, festivities kicked off around the four o'clock hour, but unlike Oprah, I was not giving away cars. I was listening to my children's confessions and what was on their minds and hearts.

On most occasions, one of them would partake in what we began to dub The Airing of the Grievances, which largely consisted of complaints about their sibling, a schoolmate, or in some cases, an existential crisis. (My children are nothing if not deep, pensive individuals.)

One particular afternoon, when my older daughter, Ruth, was in middle school, she announced that she had something to tell me. I could tell from her tone that it was serious, and I invited her to sit down and tell me what was on her mind.

"Mama, I'm gay."

I nodded in acknowledgment and told her, "I love you no matter who you love. I'm glad you know who you are, and I am grateful that you knew you could tell me."

I also knew what she was about to say next.

"Mama, can you tell Dada?"

"Of course, honey. I will tell him. I know his answer will be the same. We love you no matter who you love."

"Thanks, Mama."

Mick came home a few hours later, and after dinner, he and I retreated to the same couch, where I broke the news to him.

"Ruth told me today that she is gay."

Typically a man of few words and even fewer emotions, I was

bracing myself for his vintage Poker Face response, maybe with a nod or, if he was particularly evocative, a slight gasp.

When I tell you that NOTHING IN LIFE could have prepared me for his response, I am by no means exaggerating.

He sat up on the edge of the couch and gestured his arm like he was making a muscle and announced, "I KNEW IT!" with the joyous conviction of someone whose football team had made a great play.

"You knew it?" I responded.

"Yes. I knew it," he replied.

"Well, as glad as I am to hear that in your 25 years in this country, you've acquired a gaydar, this is not the response I was expecting."

"I can't believe YOU didn't know!"

"Listen, I have not given ONE IOTA OF THOUGHT to our 14-year-old's sexual identity, so I'm not sure what you think I've been missing."

"Well, I'm still surprised," he said.

Life continued for a few months, during which time Ruth had one brief romance with a girl named Cora. Then, nary a word about any love interest was spoken until about three months into her freshman year of high school.

Once again, on the infamous Confessional Couch, Ruth gave me the news.

"Mama, I have a boyfriend. His name is Daniel, and we are going to be Facebook Official soon," she noted solemnly and with gravitas. "I wanted to let you know."

"That's wonderful, honey. Remember, we love you no matter who you love. Would you like me to tell Dada?"

"Yes, please. It's awkward to tell him."

"That's okay. I understand. I'll let him know. We'd like to meet Daniel. He's welcome here whenever you'd like."

That evening, Mick and I shared a cup of tea at the dinner

table, and I gave him the Romance Update.

"Ruth has a boyfriend. His name is Daniel. They will be Facebook Official soon," I reported with the neutrality of an NPR newscaster.

It was at this moment that I decided that Mick needed his own spin-off series called *Mick Says the Darndest Things* because without missing a beat, he replied:

"I thought she was a full-time lesbian."

"As opposed to a part-time one? It's not a profession. She's not in a union."

"But what about being a lesbian? I thought she was a lesbian. I told everyone she's a lesbian."

I'm not sure if he thought we should issue a press release or take out an ad in *The Boston Globe*.

"I don't know, Mick. All I know is that she is willing to tell us these things, and we should be grateful for that. I don't care if she wants to be in a relationship with a dinosaur, as long as she's happy."

"What are we going to do now?"

"We are going to love her no matter who she loves."

A few months later, Ruth and Daniel broke up. She initiated it, but you could tell her heart was broken.

"It's never going to be the same, Mama," she whimpered as I held her on the Confessional Couch.

"Probably not," I said, "but you'll love other people in this life, and they will love you."

Not long after Ruth's fifteenth birthday, she initiated a new tradition, The Confessional Phone Call. She called me at my office to inform me, "Mama, I feel most comfortable in my body when I identify as a lesbian."

"I bet you do. Remember, I love you no matter who you love, sweetheart. I'm always grateful when you tell me how you feel and what you're thinking. And before you ask, I already know: You want me to tell Dada."

"Thanks, Mama."

I got home from work, plopped down on the couch, and awaited Mick's arrival.

He barely crossed the threshold when I announced, "THIS JUST IN! Ruth has been welcomed back into the fold and has retained Full-Time Lesbian status. They gave her a pension, a dental plan, and a great match on her 401(k). All of our friends who claimed their points for recruiting her to the other side now qualify for a cruise."

"Why are you making fun of me? Is this because I said 'Full-Time Lesbian?'"

"If you have to ask, then you probably already know the answer, Mick."

Over the next few years, Ruth continued to explore the complicated world of attraction, lust, love, first dates, break-ups, and everything in between. At times, she'd swear off relationships altogether, claiming, "I need to work on me." Other times, she brought someone home but wouldn't disclose the relationship beyond "a friend." In between, she plopped onto my Oprah Couch to vent or sob or get motherly advice (which she typically ignored, as children are wont to do!).

And then one day, another announcement...

"I am going by Rueben now, and I prefer the pronouns they/them."

By this time, Mick and I had separated, and I was living across town. I knew from her tone that she told him first, a milestone in and of itself.

"I love you no matter what," I replied as we sat across from each other in my kitchen.

So now, as another chapter in the story of Rueben's life begins, and they become who they are, our family mantra has expanded to "We love you no matter who you love, what name you call yourself, or what pronouns you want to go by."

Radical acceptance. Unconditional love. That's all I can offer, and it's precisely what they need.

I don't know where Rueben's story will go from here. Perhaps they'll circle back in a few years with another Family Bulletin and announce that their identity has shifted subtly, or dramatically, once again. And that's fine by me.

Because the thing is, nobody ever stays completely the same. We all change. We all try on certain identities to see if they fit, and sometimes they do, and sometimes not quite. I've gone through plenty of evolutions myself. I was single, then married, then divorced. I was Harrington, then McLaughlin, now back to Harrington again. I had a job, then I was self-employed, and now I'm taking a crack at writing books. I trust that my family will love me throughout all the evolutions of life, and I will extend that same acceptance to each of them.

I would be more disturbed if my children never ever changed one bit. Now THAT would be troubling.

Loud Monkey

My Brother, Charlie H., sent me a text this morning that reminded me of another epic story involving Our Father, Bill H.

The tale of "Loud Monkey."

In keeping with our family's theme of finding humor in the darnedest places, this story takes place at a funeral, namely Bill H.'s.

Bill H.'s demise a week following his fifty-sixth birthday did not come as a surprise to any of us. He smoked and drank at a rate that could only be described as "competitive" and "in direct defiance of doctor's orders."

Bill H. attempted to get sober several times, going to AA meetings and generally making our lives miserable in a host of new and exciting ways. His signature way to torture our mother was by collecting his fellow meeting members like stray dogs and bringing them to our house for a post-meeting meal. Mary H. always obliged, reasoning that at least Bill H. wasn't at a bar drinking his paycheck away.

On the day of Bill H.'s funeral services, one of the first things we speculated about was who from this cast of characters would make it to pay respects at the funeral home.

"I'm not sure they know he's dead," said my mother, "after all, he's not been to a meeting for years."

"Trust me," I replied, "God has a wicked sense of humor. One of them will show up, and we won't ever forget about it."

Almost seconds after my prediction, a small man in a cap and trenchcoat approached the doorway of the grieving room. He stopped, looked both ways as if he were being followed, then quickly signed the condolences book. He walked right past us to the casket, jumped back, and ran out of the room.

More curious than shocked, I followed him out to see if I could speak with him, but he was practically sprinting out of the funeral home.

I turned to look at the condolences book to find out his name.

All I could decipher from the scrawl?

Loud Monkey.

The two words my brother sends me every year on the anniversary of our father's burial.

Fake Birthday

You know the saying "Desperate times call for desperate measures?" Well, that basically was my parenting mantra when my kids were small.

I worked part-time, and they were in daycare three days a week. This arrangement was great until Ruth hit kindergarten, refused to take the bus to school, and Zoe was still in preschool. Add to the mix the fact we had moved to a different end of town that was equidistant to Ru's school and Zoe's preschool, and suddenly I found myself commuting an hour a day to work at home.

To add to the misery (because why stop there?) Zoe's preschool was experiencing some growing pains: There had been a large staff turnover, and for a child who hated change, drop-off had become a nightmare: crying, screaming, begging to leave. Zoe didn't do well either.

Where was my husband during all this? Who the fuck knows? This was the height of my career as Married Single Mom, but I'm not bitter or anything.

But I digress...

My next step was to do what I do best: find solutions in the darnedest places. And by that, I mean I stopped in a new daycare that I passed en route to bring Ruth to school and basically begged for a spot.

It worked! They offered me a threee-day-a-week spot right there. I'm sure it had nothing to do with the crazed look in my eyes.

Now I just had to sell Zoe on this idea.

I took her to visit the classroom the next day, explaining that she was a big girl and was going to get to go to a new preschool!

"I don't want to go to a new preschool."

"Well, this one has a teacher that is nice and is going to stay longer than a week!"

"I don't want to leave my friends."

"You will still have your friends, and you'll make new ones!"

"I don't wanna."

"Let's just visit."

When we arrived, we were greeted not only by her teachers but by two little girls who began interrogating me.

"What's her name?"

"Zoe."

"Why won't she talk to us?"

"She will. She's just getting used to the new space."

"So we should leave her alone?"

"Maybe for today."

Then Zoe made the announcement that indicated she could possibly tolerate the new place.

"I need to go potty," she said.

And off we went, to the place where all of Zoe's great thinking takes place.

As she sat on the potty, she looked at me and said, "I will come here for school. But not until I am four years old."

Now I thought this was pretty clever. She wanted to bargain.

But I was desperate. She couldn't transition well with all the upheaval at her current preschool, and I couldn't sustain driving all over town to work at home.

So, once again, I found a solution in the most unexpected place: my imagination.

"Well, aren't you lucky! Your birthday is on Friday!"

(So what if it was four weeks early?)

"It is?!?!"

"Yes! It is!!"

"I can't wait!"

"Me either!!!" (Clearly.)

She bought it. We decided right then and there, while washing hands, that we would celebrate with her current preschool class on Friday by bringing cupcakes. Then she would be four and could go to her new school on Monday.

We marched proudly out of the bathroom and announced our plans to her new teachers, who, bless them, went right along with my desperate hair-brained scheme like a troupe of improv artists.

The old preschool was so shell-shocked by my announcement that they went along with it out of pure amazement.

When Zoe's actual birthday came, I brought in cupcakes to celebrate her first month with new friends.

"Why do I have two birthdays?"

"Oh, why make your new friends wait until you're five? Cupcakes for everyone!"

And so the very first Fake Birthday came and went, and soon enough, it was all but forgotten by both Zoe and me. (I'm not sure Mick ever knew about it, to be honest.)

That was until another Zoe entered the picture. Zoe P.

Zoe P. and our Zoe became friends in early elementary school and rode the bus together to and from school. Zoe's mom, Jenn, and I became fast friends as well. But the real star of the show in Zoe P.'s life was her grandfather, Papouli, who was often the person picking up Zoe P. at the bus stop after school.

If you've ever had to pick up kids at a bus stop, you know that it quickly becomes a sort of airport lounge, where everyone gets to know each other, not only as parents but as people. Papouli had emigrated to the United States in the late 1960s and had recently retired following a career that spanned everything from owning a pizza shop to working for a fire alarm company.

But the fact about Papouli that stands out most to me is that Papouli also had a fake birthday.

In what was some sort of mix-up in his immigration process,

the month and date of Papouli's birthday were transposed (mostly likely due to European-style DDMMYY vs. the American MMD-DYY). If memory serves, his real birthday is November 4, but some of his paperwork states it is April 11.

I learned about Papouli's fake birthday from our eight-year-old Zoe, who, apropos of absolutely nothing, announced it while doing homework at the kitchen table.

"Mama, Papouli has a FAKE BIRTHDAY! Jenn and Zoe P. have a cake and everything for him!"

As Zoe regaled me with what (to her) was a tale of wonder, I reminisced about Zoe's own fake birthday, which I contend is my Greatest Mothering Hack. Caught up in nostalgia and my own smug triumph, I made the rare mistake of blurting out the reply, "Oh, you have a fake birthday too, honey."

"I do?" said Zoe, incredulous that she could have something in common with Papouli.

"Oh yes, I gave you a fake birthday so you would go to a new preschool. You told me you'd only go there when you turned four, so I told you your birthday was earlier than it really was," I replied nonchalantly, as if this were an everyday occurrence, like "all the moms are doing it."

"When is my fake birthday?"

"January 30."

"So, you lied to me about my birthday?" Zoe said forlornly but with a hint of mischief. I could all but hear the wheels turning in her head as to how she would use this information as leverage.

"Well, in absolute terms, yes. I lied. But I did so because you were having a tough time at your preschool, and I knew you needed a new environment. Now I'm not going to lie: I also did so because commuting across town between Ruth's school and your preschool was a struggle for me too. Moms do things sometimes that are in the interest of the whole family, including the moms."

"Can we celebrate my fake birthday?" Zoe is nothing if not food-motivated.

"Sure. Why not. What kind of cake do you want? We don't even have to wait until January; we can do it whenever."

Ruth, who had up to this point been quietly sitting on the sidelines, quickly interjected. "What about me? Why can't I have a fake birthday?"

"No one said you can't have a fake birthday. What day do you want yours?"

"St. Patrick's Day," she replied.

"Fine, mark the calendar, so no one forgets."

"Are YOU going to have a fake birthday too, Mama?" Zoe asked.

"Sure, I'll pick July 4 because I already feel like my birthday should be a national holiday, so I'll piggyback on our nation's birthday."

"What about Dada? Does he even KNOW about the fake birthdays? Will HE get a fake birthday?" Ruth asked.

"Honestly, I have no idea if he even knows about the origin of this whole fake birthday thing, so how about we get a cake and surprise him with the news?"

That was the year Zoe turned 8 and 9, Ru aged from 10 to 11, and I remained 39. I am forever young, after all.

And Mick? Well, the irony with him is that he has to be reminded when his real birthday is. In the first year of the Fake Birthdays Reprise, he turned 51 yet felt 92 trying to keep up with my parenting-by-the-seat-of-my-pants approach.

Parenting: building the plane as you fly it.

Endings and Beginnings

While I've been blessed with a lifetime of great stories from the family I was born into and the family I made, I'm embarking on a chapter that's both an ending and a beginning: my divorce from Mick.

If you've been through a divorce, you know that you don't wake up one day and say, "Okay, today I'm going to Target, the supermarket, and a divorce attorney."

Nor is divorce prompted by a singular event; it's more like death by a thousand tiny cuts that start as pinpricks on your heart. Kisses offered like handshakes; obligatory, without passion. Gradually, there are words that sting, then actions that sear. You dismiss the evolution with aphorisms like, "Oh, we're having a rough time; this too shall pass."

Yeah. Like a kidney stone.

Before you know it, you feel like you're bleeding on yourself and everyone around you.

There's so much I could say about why and how my marriage to Mick fell into pieces. There's, of course, the pithy phrase "We grew apart." And that's true.

What's more true is an adage I heard years ago but somehow never thought would apply to me: Women marry men thinking that the men will change, and they never do. Men marry women thinking they'll never change, and they always do.

While I don't necessarily believe I wanted Mick to change, I did expect that we would grow as humans as the years pressed on. I also don't think Mick thought I would be exactly the same person I was the day he met me in 1996, but I'm not sure he was prepared for how much I would evolve over our 25 years together.

My friend Julie's mother offered stark advice on the morning of Julie's sister's wedding: "Marry him for his faults because that's all you'll have left in the end."

Dark as fuck? You bet it is. Yet the moment Julie shared these words with me (over copious amounts of wine as I cried and mourned my failed marriage), I realized the root of Mick's and my struggle. Our faults were no longer bearable and birthed a shared intolerance that grew into our mutual disdain for one another.

Mick's steady presence was what drew me to him. After a childhood of turmoil and trauma, all I sought in a partner was consistency. Mick possessed that in spades. You can set a clock by Mick; he wakes up at the same time every morning and goes about his routine with the precision of a Swiss watch. I often joked that he is the kind of guy who says, "It's 12 o'clock; I must be hungry."

But, as the saying goes, "familiarity breeds contempt." Over time, I began to see Mick's consistency as stubbornness, resistance to change, and blind faith in routine that I found, at best, befuddling; at worst, downright infuriating.

The very thing that initially impressed me and attracted me to him—his consistency—became the trait I loathed the most.

The essence of Mick is that he is an enigma wrapped up in a puzzle; it's hard to know what he's thinking. He's at best economical with his words; at worst, non-verbal. But I'd venture to guess that he initially admired my ambition, my sense of adventure, and my yearning for new experiences. Yet, as the years wore on, he viewed those traits as my incapability of appreciating the simple things, a fundamental dissatisfaction with life as we built it.

He wasn't wrong. I grew to feel like I had put my life on hold for our family's benefit, that I shoehorned my life around everyone else's needs, and I was deeply unhappy. As Meryl Streep's character, Francesca Johnson, says in *The Bridges of Madison County*:

"You become a mother, a wife, and you stop and stay steady so that your children can move. And when they leave, they take your life of details with them."

I could not stay steady. I wanted my own life with my own details. My longing turned into resentment and was at a constant simmer. As the years wore on, the simmer grew to a wave of boiling anger that grew bigger and bigger until it swallowed us all.

Parting ways seemed the only solution, and it was Mick who initiated our separation. I'd always said that Mick rarely voiced an opinion, so when he did, I was inclined to not only listen but defer to him.

Ironically, the only other time I recall him expressing a deeply-held belief was when he insisted that I take his name in marriage. I had no intention of converting my name from Harrington to McLaughlin, but Mick simply said, "It means a lot to me that we share a name," so in what to me was the ultimate act of love, I became Judi McLaughlin.

We are still figuring out what kind of relationship we want to maintain with one another and how best to support our children. It's tricky and wrought with emotion. I don't wish this dynamic on anyone, but I know that this deeply dysfunctional time isn't happening to us; it's happening for us.

And it's made me realize that while Mick and I were meant to be together, we were not meant to stay together.

I will always remember our "lost in translation" moments and laugh, especially the term "wee beastie," his catch-all phrase for backyard vermin, or my personal favorite, "arse-washer," his term for a bidet.

I will always be grateful for the family we made together and the family he made me a part of. How his late dad, Big John, welcomed me with a bone-crushing hug and dubbed me Jo-Jo. (Nothing in Mick's family says "I love you" like giving you a nickname.)

I hit the lottery in knowing his mom, Sadie, the World's Greatest Mother-in-Law, who loves me unconditionally and celebrated my brand of motherhood in spite of it not always aligning with hers.

I'm blessed with a gaggle of nieces and nephews who I also count as my dearest friends. My niece, Caroline, who cared for my brood as babies and serves as "other mother" to them now, and who gave me one of my greatest titles: godmother. Her son, Cahir, is a light in my life whose wit is only surpassed by his kindness.

And, of course, my Kevin, the Nephew Who Loved Me First.

I will hold Mick's demonstrations of love forever in my heart, even the unusual ones—a microwave, a TV, a stereo, a vacuum cleaner—because I know his intentions were good.

The unhappiness in our marriage was real. But all of those sweet moments were equally real. Both/and.

As Dr. Seuss, the Patron Author of the Harrington Family, once said, "Don't be sad that it's over. Be happy that it happened."

What I have come to understand is that every relationship comes to an end, one way or another. It always begins. It always ends.

You meet someone. You feel a spark. You fall in love. And then, one day, it is over.

Maybe it ends due to infidelity, disdain, contempt, or all three. Maybe it ends because one person wants to move to Indiana for a job and the other does not. Maybe it ends because someone dies of cancer, or there's a terrible car crash, or someone slips getting out of the shower while reaching for their phone to see a 20% off Groupon code.

The relationship might last 2 months or 20 years or 50, but sooner or later, it's going to end.

So perhaps, we can accept this fact—it always begins, and it always ends. Instead of fearing the inevitable ending, perhaps we can squeeze every possible drop of life and love out of the time we've got together.

Maybe our wedding vows ought to go, "Hey, I know this

relationship will end eventually, one way or another, but while we're at it? I will bring you the best of me every day. And some days, I will fail miserably. But I swear on the Red Sox, I will try."

Acknowledgments

Am I the only one who's dreamed of what they would say if they were to give an Oscar acceptance speech?

Just me? Okay.

Anyway, "giving an Oscar-style speech" has always been on my Bucket List, and this book is The Next Best Thing, so here goes:

First, I would like to thank Jesus for turning water into wine because I certainly consumed my fair share in writing this book.

Next, I would like to thank Juan Valdez and coffee farmers across the globe for The Elixir of Life, Caffeine. Without them, I am nothing.

Speaking of "I am nothing," THIS BOOK would be nothing if not for Alexandra Franzen and Lindsey Smith at Get It Done, LLC. When I submitted my manuscript to Get It Done, Alex and Lindsey immediately "got" me in ways I didn't even know needed to be understood.

I also want to thank Christina Frei of The Innate Marketing Genius for introducing me to Alex and Lindsey. Christina, you are one of the great surprises of my life. If not for you, I'd never have met Alex, Lindsey, and the Get It Done team. I am forever grateful to you.

A note of thanks to my parents, Bill H. and Mary H. Bill H., I've lived my life longer without you than with you, and while you were batshit crazy on this earth, you taught me so much about how to call bullshit and the power of storytelling. Mary H., you may not have always agreed with my path, but you remained faithful that I knew what the hell I was doing, even when I was unsure myself.

To my brother, Charlie H.: You may have been the first

published author in the family, but my book is way funnier.

I would NOT like to thank my was-bund, Mick McLaughlin. However, in the interest of fairness (and, for the record, I hate to be fair), he did create two exceptional humans with me. Without our children, there'd be no stories called "My Jewish Kid" or "Zoe's Imaginary Family and Friends and Fellow Inmates."

Mick, I'm not sure you always appreciated my sense of humor or my comedic timing. Alas, the struggle of living and loving alongside someone whose poker face rivals that of New England Patriots coach Bill Belichick. You just don't know how they feel.

That said: Mick, I hope these stories make you laugh deep down inside, where it counts the most.

If not, then you can have the last Rolo.

Finally, if I did not thank you in this book, please keep your complaints to yourself.

Thank you for attending my Ted Talk.

Author Bio

Judi Harrington was born in Boston, Massachusetts, and grew up in Fall River, MA.

She is a proud graduate of the University of Massachusetts-Boston, where she earned a Bachelor of Arts in English Composition and Professional Writing and fell deeply in love with the Oxford English Dictionary and Computational Linguistics.

Judi holds a Master of Arts degree from Emerson College in Organizational Communication and Management (she doesn't know what this means either, so please don't ask).

She served 15 years of hard time in the corporate trenches of Putnam Investments, Thomson-Reuters, Fidelity Management & Research Co., and a myriad of law offices throughout the Boston area before founding her own copywriting business, Judi 411 (www.judi411.com), in 2019.

Fuckery: The Life and Times of a Legend (in Her Own Mind) is Judi's first book.

CPSIA information can be obtained
at www.ICGtesting.com
Printed in the USA
BVHW052251161022
649595BV00004B/108